COMMENTARY ON THE HOLY WAR

SOUNDING THE TRUMPET AT THE EAR-GATE.

COMMENTARY

ON

JOHN BUNYAN'S

THE HOLY WAR

MADE BY KING SHADDAI UPON DIABOLUS, FOR THE REGAINING
OF THE METROPOLIS OF THE WORLD; OR THE LOSING AND
TAKING AGAIN OF THE TOWN OF MANSOUL.

BY

REV. ROBERT MAGUIRE, M. A.

COMPILED BY
CHARLES J. DOE

A PUBLICATION OF

CURIOSMITH

MINNEAPOLIS
2009

PUBLISHER'S NOTE

The annotations of John Bunyan's, *The Holy War*, were compiled from the footnotes of an edition published by Cassell, Petter, and Galpin, c. 1863. Each chapter begins with an outline of major events to guide readers. *The Holy War* text phrase is in script, which is followed by the corresponding notes and commentary. All notes are maintained in the same chapter and same order they appeared.

Published by Curiosmith.
P. O. Box 390293, Minneapolis, Minnesota, 55439.
Internet: curiosmith.com.
E-mail: shopkeeper@curiosmith.com.

All footnotes are added by the publisher.

ISBN 978-0-9817505-7-6

Library of Congress Control Number: 2009931663

CONTENTS

INTRODUCTION

In the HOLY WAR we have one of the choicest of the Allegorical Works of the immortal BUNYAN. Compared with his PILGRIM'S PROGRESS, it is an Allegory of quite a different style and character, presenting another phase of the soul's experience. Bunyan's HOLY WAR, in fact, may properly be called "A History of the Human Soul."

In this respect, the present Allegory differs from the former work of "the Glorious Dreamer:" the PILGRIM'S PROGRESS dealt with the external circumstances of the Christian Pilgrimage, as they were helpful to, or obstructive of the spiritual life; and thence proceeded to the inner experiences of the Christian. The HOLY WAR deals with the inward struggles of the soul, and thence proceeds to the outer consequences, as they affect the peace and happiness of man. The PILGRIM'S PROGRESS describes the enemies from without, affecting the soul within; while the HOLY WAR describes the enemies from within, affecting the whole life and fortune of the man.

For these reasons many have regarded the Allegory of the HOLY WAR as a more spiritual work than even the PILGRIM'S PROGRESS; and, perhaps, on this account it has been less appreciated by the general public. This instructive Allegory is a dissector of the heart, in the spiritual anatomy of the soul. It is a spiritual mirror, setting forth what man was, whose servant he has become, what wars and fightings, what struggles and conflicts must be waged and utterly fought out, before Christ is again enthroned, and Mansoul Lost can sing the new song, worthy of Mansoul Regained. O Lord ♡

The two great ideas that prevail throughout the work are those of Mansoul Lost and Mansoul Recovered; reminding us of Milton's two great Works—"Paradise Lost" and "Paradise Regained." The first allusion to the town of Mansoul refers to the soul of man in general, in the abstract—that essence, called the soul, man's being, on which God's image and superscription once reposed. It was God's workmanship; and, like all God's works, it was pronounced "very good." It was, of all created things, the nearest in resemblance, and the dearest in affection, to God himself: "in the image of God created he man." The soul was made to be God's dwelling-place, the habita-

tion of his seat. The citadel of Mansoul is the heart; the walls, the
body or the flesh; and the gates, the five senses—hence their suggestive names. The inhabitants of the town are the understanding,
the conscience, the will, the hopes, the joys, the thoughts—the
thousand thoughts that crowd within the soul; these are the men,
the women, and the children of the town, conceived, and brought
forth, fostered, and thus growing into deeds for good or for evil. This
palace of the King fell into the designing hands of Satan (DIABOLUS)
and his captains; illustrating the words of the wise man—that sad
compendium of all human history—"Lo, this only have I found, that
God hath made man upright; but they have sought out many
inventions" (Ecclesiastes 7:29).

This sad extremity of fallen Mansoul is accepted as God's glorious opportunity. This breach of the holy covenant between God and
man at once engages the Son of God in the interest of his fallen
creature. IMMANUEL now covenants with his Father that he will
himself reclaim the soul to the sovereignty of God; and this he
accomplishes by his death and sacrifice, and the subsequent dealings and operations of his Spirit. O Lord O

But, meanwhile, Satan has set up his throne in Mansoul, and
established a new government there. The usurper must be dislodged. Accordingly the struggle begins (and here the Allegory
descends to particulars—to your soul or mine). The soul is re-taken
by Christ; but there are still the lurking Diabolonians, the seed of
the evil heart, the residue of the tares, the remnant of the "old man"
and the corrupt nature. These ofttimes cause spiritual damage to
the soul; they grieve the Holy Spirit; and sometimes drive Christ
away from the occupancy of the throne. Satan soon enters, and
must again be dislodged. These alternating fortunes of the great
fight of faith are the phases of our own spiritual life, leaving us
either nearer to Christ or farther from him than before.

Such is the nature of this inimitable work—THE HOLY WAR. We
would bespeak the attention of the godly and the ungodly, the free
child of God and the bond-servant of Satan, the weak believer and
the trembling, doubting Christian, to this marvelous exposition of
the "battle of the warrior!"

CHAPTER I

MANSOUL: ITS ORIGIN AND FALL

OUTLINE OF CHAPTER I.—Description of its Original State.—
Shaddai, its King.—Its Castle and Walls.—The Five Gates of the
Town.—Nature of its Provisions and Defenses.—The Character of
its Inhabitants, and the Secret of its Safety.—Diabolus: his
Origin.—His Ambition and Pride.—His Fall.—His Spirit of Re-
venge.—His Design on Mansoul.—Council of War.—The Assault.—
Death of Captains Resistance and Innocency.—Mr. Understanding
and Mr. Conscience removed from Office.—The Lord Will-be-will
promoted.—Shaddai Dishonored.—The New Mayor, Recorder, and
Aldermen of Mansoul.—The Strongholds of Satan.

The continent of Universe.—The Allegorist assumes the wide scope
of universal nature as his field of observation in this wondrous
narrative. When the great "Dreamer" conceived his great subject in
his "den" at Bedford, his eye took in only the continuous path of the
"narrow way," along which his Pilgrim or his Pilgrims travelled to
their distant home; but now he takes a wider range, a more exten-
sive scope, even "the famous continent of Universe." In such a field
of observation, the astronomer would search for stars, and suns,
and systems; the philosopher would seek for morals, and mysteries,
and metaphysical subtleties; the lover of nature would dig for
hidden pearls in all its recesses; the biographer would fix his eye
upon master-minds and men of parts, who stand amid the common
crowd, head and shoulders above other men. But the poor tinker of
Elstow can see and contemplate nought else within that space than
this *human nature* of ours, fallen thus deep, degraded so low; and
seeing this, he writes the biography of MAN.

A town called Mansoul.—Yes, the Soul is the all-engaging object of
the writer's contemplation; it is first, last—everything. He can see
nothing so great in its inestimable loss, if it be lost; nothing so
grand in its inestimable gain, if it be saved; nothing so wide, so vast,
so unutterably immeasurable, when viewed in the light of eternity
to come—an eternity of misery and woe, or else of happiness and

bliss. The soul seemed to him, as it stood forth, the one great object in space, ever visible, never hidden or obscured, seen in the light and gleaming in the darkness, tending toward the days that are to be, creating the future while it is transacting the present, with heaven above and hell beneath, to live for ever or for ever to die! He contemplates the struggle:—Satan's triumphs, and then the triumphs of Immanuel, the loss and the gain, the alternating victory and defeat; and fixing his eyes intently on his object, he writes the History of the HOLY WAR!

The position of Mansoul was "between the two worlds," just the position of the Pilgrim in the former Allegory, whose Progress was "from this world to that which is to come."

The Architect and Builder of the town was one SHADDAI. This is God's all-powerful name, indicative of his greatness, glory, and all-mightiness—"the pourer forth."

The walls and gates were impregnable from without. The continuance of security was lodged in the hands of the inhabitants. The town was the palace of King SHADDAI, and could not be wrested from his dominion, "unless the townsmen gave consent thereto." It was not the destiny of heaven, nor the subtlety of hell, nor yet the book of fate and inevitable doom, that could open the gates of Mansoul but only man's own will and choice.

> "God made thee perfect, not immutable;
> And good he made thee; but to persevere
> He left it in thy pow'r; ordained thy will,
> By nature, free."[*]

One Diabolus.—The word "Diabolus," from the Greek, has the same meaning as the Hebrew word "Satan." It is differently rendered, "slanderer," "accuser," "adversary."

How sin came to be; how the spirit of evil entered heaven, and succeeded in alienating holy and perfect beings from truth and righteousness, is a mystery still hid in God, and only partially revealed to us. There has been much of curious and unprofitable speculation, both in poetry and prose, as to the origin of evil. The Bible is the only source from whence we gather any reliable information on a subject so mysterious. Satan, now the prince of the devils, was very likely once a chief over a legion of angels, a hierarch in heaven, having under his command "thrones, dominations, princedoms, virtues, powers." This leader and his host rebelled, and for their

---

[*]John Milton, *Paradise Lost,* 1667.

rebellion they were cast out. Two passages of Scripture comprise all that we know upon this subject—2 Peter 2:4, and Jude 6. What more we know of Satan, we know by our own experience, by his indwelling and inworking in our hearts, and in the world around us.

All, and always Eye.—This is the expressive form in which Bunyan states the omniscience and omnipresence of Deity, which twain attributes, when followed up by the power of his omnipotence, discovered the conspiracy, and defeated the conspirators. Ambition was their sin, and rebellion the result. There was war in heaven; Satan was vanquished in the fight, and driven from the seats of bliss into deep perdition and unutterable loss. There he lay, "confounded, though immortal." Even there his spirit was not quenched. The "unconquerable will," and "study of revenge," "immortal hate," and "courage never to submit or yield,"—all these remained, as the bases of new plots, revolutions, and rebellions, which soon found scope enough, in this "continent of Universe," against the town of Mansoul.

A Council of War.—Devils hold conclave, and speak their mind, as wrath, or hate, or wily policy dictates. Unable to climb to heaven again, and loth to brook submission in their fall, they voted an assault on Mansoul—that holy, happy, innocent place, where Godlike man, the image of his Maker, dwelt. This met with universal approval, was hailed with shouts of joy, and Pandemonium echoed to the sound.

Sat down before Ear-gate.—This was the gate of audience, and through this gate the words of the tempter must penetrate, if the temptation is to be successful. Into the ears of our first mother did the wily serpent whisper the glozing words of his seductive wiles; and through Ear-gate he assailed her heart, and won it. To give audience to the tempter is the next step to yielding up obedience to his will.

And Mansoul hearkens to the words of Satan. The principal inhabitants of the town give him audience; that is, the ruling powers and chief attributes of the soul are content to hold a parley with Satan. His words are words of courtesy, a plausible harangue. With all his deceit and guile, he promises to enlarge their town, to increase their knowledge, to augment their freedom; and for this he doth belie their King. The one forbidden thing, which was intended to be their test, he makes to be their very temptation. He urges the want of proportion between the forbidden offence, and the threatened punishment. He did even chide the townsmen with their egregious folly, that the fruit is calculated to make them wise, and yet they dare not eat of it!

Mansoul is attracted, and lends an ear. Thus the first step is gained; and while the tempter thus plausibly prolongs his speech, an arrow is dispatched from the string of the fury, and Captain RESISTANCE falls. "Resist the devil, and he will flee from you;" but if he once beats down the spirit of man's resistance, he draws to close quarters, and soon attains the mastery.

Mr. Ill-pause.—This man, the orator of DIABOLUS, is intended to represent halting and hesitation of the soul, while it stays to listen to the tempter. Satan has many mysterious angels who are ready to second their master's temptations, and to commend his wily overtures. Thus ILL-PAUSE persuades the men of Mansoul; and, lo! to the temptation from without (which was utterly powerless in itself), there answers the yielding from within. This is the fatal act; and is straightway followed by another grave disaster—the death of INNOCENCY, one of the chiefest and most honorable townsmen. His sensitive soul was poisoned by the contact of the breath of the lost. Keep innocence secure, for it is easily offended and made weak; it is a delicate plant, that finds it hard to hold its own amid the pollution and defilement of this naughty world.

So they opened the gates.—The beauty and the strength, the two pillars of the state, of Mansoul have fallen. For Resistance, we read Weakness, and for Innocency, we read Ichabod—its glory and its might departed in one day: and there is now no more strength left. They have hearkened to the Tempter's words—*Ear*-gate is assailed! They deem the tree to be good for food—*Feel*-gate yields! The fruit is pleasant to the eye—*Eye*-gate bends its strength! It is to be desired to make one wise—the *heart* now covets the forbidden thing! At last, Mansoul plucked the fruit, and ate it, and knew not that it was eating *death*.

Diabolus marches to the middle.—Whatever advantage is gained by Satan, he is sure to make use of for ulterior ends. He reckons that he has accomplished nothing until he has attained the castle, the citadel of Mansoul—that is, the heart. He that is master there, commands the town and all its outworks.

"Alas! my poor Mansoul!"—Satan here speaks to Mansoul from within; but how different is his speech now! In his former harangue, delivered outside the walls, he had undervalued SHADDAI'S power; now he magnifies it. Outside, he had urged the townsmen to despise Jehovah's counsel; now, from within, he urges them to defend themselves against his wrath. There is a vast difference between the argument and attitude of DIABOLUS outside and inside the soul. Outside the walls he is plausible, fair-spoken, and even beseeching;

inside, he is peremptory, authoritative, and commanding. Outside, he lies to man, and belies the King; inside, he (to some extent) speaks the truth. He truthfully enough reports the power and wrath of SHADDAI; and thereby endeavors to put Mansoul in a state of defense, and even of defiance, against its lawful King, while he enslaves its inhabitants and robs them of their glory.

New-modeling the town.—Consistently with the possession of the heart by Satan, we now find that all is changed to his will, and conformed to his purpose. Mansoul has lost its Divine and heavenly strength; so now it is made strong with the strength of hell. When the soul forfeits the protection of Jehovah, it places itself under the protection of the Wicked One. Not one stone of its former strength and constitution is left upon another; all is altered and new-modeled to the will of the tyrant.

The great and high dignitaries of Mansoul were as the town itself; as is the constituency, so is the representation. Its chief inhabitants, once holy and innocent, are now fallen and debased. Understanding and Conscience are the first to suffer. Such is the gratitude of DIABOLUS to those that serve him! He had promised enlarged dominion, increase of knowledge, and augmented freedom. The first and immediate result is—the loss of dominion; the increase of knowledge is the knowledge of their loss; and for the promised freedom they receive but bondage.

The Lord Mayor, Understanding.—The Understanding is the lord and umpire of the soul, holding the intellectual mastery over man. This power, having once a far-seeing eye, a quick perception, an understanding heart, and a lordly counsel, is now degraded, darkened, and imprisoned, "having the understanding darkened," Ephesians 4:18.

The Recorder.—Conscience is the memory of the heart, the moral memory of man, the recorder of the soul. This ruling power of Mansoul, having consented to the entrance of DIABOLUS, must now reap as it hath sown. The Fall has more than doubled the work of Conscience; for it has now not only to remember the height of glory from whence it has fallen, but also to preserve the records of its present degradation. Conscience is the detector of the heart, the ready-reckoner of the soul. A man's conscience is his very self; he may escape from others, but he can never escape from himself. Men would banish Conscience to a far-off land, but he cleaves all the more closely to them still; they would drown it in the deep, but only to find that many waters cannot quench it; they would intoxicate it with the wine-cup, but only to be bound again in stronger bondage; they would bury the dead out of their sight, but the dead past *will not* be buried, but ever rises again in a daily resurrection, washed up on the wave of thought, exhumed from the grave of forgetfulness, by the unresting power of this inward monitor. Conscience is the undying exercise of memory here, and will be the immortality of remembrance hereafter.

My Lord Willbewill.—The Will of man has always been a high ruling power in Mansoul. It once served under SHADDAI; it now is the viceroy of DIABOLUS. It is the Will of man that determines and decides. It was this headstrong, self-willed, obdurate power that first yielded to the assault of Satan, and opened the gates of the town. And now he scorns to be a slave, and must still bear rule in Mansoul. Accordingly, the Will yielded itself to Satan; and Satan, having subjugated the human Will to his own absolute authority, promoted it to high office in the body, a threefold office: as captain of the Castle—the *heart*; governor of the walls—the *flesh*; and keeper of the gates—the *senses*. Such is the full dominion of the Will ruling through the heart, the flesh, and the senses.

One Mr. Mind for his clerk.—All the associations of the Will are consistent with its present depraved condition. The Mind is subject to the Will. As the Will dictates, so the Mind conceives and brings forth its thoughts, and develops them into deeds. The Will that is itself perverse will be sure to pervert the mind. Thus the joint action of the Will and the Mind in the service of Satan is for the uprooting of all holy principles, the casting away of the last small remnant of God's word treasured up in the soul, the darkening of every gleam of light that dawns upon the understanding, and the violent resistance to the calls and admonitions of the conscience of man.

A Deputy, Mr. Affection.—When the affections serve the carnal Will, they are perverted into *vile* affections. Under such direction, the emotions of the soul become the promptings of evil. Nor do they abide alone, but become prolific of a cursed progeny. When Affection is wedded to Lust, the offspring will be a Diabolonian brood. There is a parentage and pedigree of sin. Sins produce sins; grow out of sins; grow into sins. Sins group themselves into families, and intermarry and propagate their kind, and reproduce themselves a thousandfold. "When lust hath conceived, it bringeth forth sin; and sin, when it is finished, bringeth forth death," James 1:15.

Betakes himself to defacing.—For the full construction of Satan's kingdom there must needs be the utter destruction of SHADDAI'S sovereignty, and all things appertaining thereto. "Whose is this image and superscription?"—these were the remnants of the former service of Mansoul; but they must now be removed, and the image and superscription of DIABOLUS set up instead thereof. Every vestige and association of the past must be erased, and clean wiped out of remembrance; for now the great DIABOLUS is King, and never yet did a usurper tolerate any memento or remembrance of the rightful sovereign.

The law of SHADDAI, too, was dishonored, and trodden under foot. License and licentiousness reigned supreme. Violence, and wrong, and robbery reveled with liberty unrestrained. Alas! God was grievously dishonored, man was shamefully debased, and Satan was heartily served.

The offices of state continued, though the former officers were removed. New ruling powers were promoted over Mansoul; their names indicating the strong contrariety between the new and the old. The authority that is set up in Mansoul is, not Mr. UNDERSTANDING, but a headless, eyeless, earless Body, all lust and passion, without reason or perception; brutish, carnal, and corrupti- ble; "given over to a reprobate mind." The once memory of the soul, the recorder of good, is now displaced; and forgetfulness of God, and of all good things, set up instead.

Now, trace and reckon up the past—Mansoul, that once fair and lovely paradise, revolted from its King, and lowly prostrate under the hoof of its oppressor! Did ever a wily general so engarrison himself; or so strongly fortify his position, or make good his chosen strongholds? How he took full possession, sealed every avenue of approach, closed every gate of access, commanded every pass, bound every soul, filled every office, defaced every trace of better days gone by! How he slew RESISTANCE, and made INNOCENCE to die; imprisoned UNDERSTANDING, and darkened the light thereof; debauched CONSCIENCE, and lulled the old Recorder into a temporary oblivion and deep slumber of sleep; perverted the Will, and made it his slave; blotted out the image of God, and turned man, as by a transforming power, from the likeness of God to the similitude of Satan; suppressed the law of God, and made it to be of none effect; set up lust, and vile affection, and carnal desire and forgetfulness of good, and the strongholds of the Wicked One, in the place of those high and holy and heavenly principles that once bare rule in Mansoul! All these combine to make up the full picture of man's fallen nature. "God be merciful to us sinners!"

CHAPTER II

PREPARATIONS AND COUNTER-PREPARATIONS

OUTLINE OF CHAPTER II.—Tidings brought to the King.—
Covenant of the King's Son.—Immanuel.—The Devices of Satan.—
The Oath of Allegiance.—Mansoul reduced to Bondage, Degrada-
tion, and Despair.—The Diabolonian Armor:—1. The Helmet of
False-peace.—2. The Iron Breastplate—the Hard Heart.—3. The
Sword—the Fiery Lying Tongue.—4. The Shield—of Unbelief.—5.
The Dumb and Prayerless Spirit.—Preparations for the Fight.

Tidings were carried to the King.—Upon a review of the circumstances
of the Fall of Mansoul, we may well say—"How are the mighty
fallen!" Our next thought, perhaps, would be—What will SHADDAI do?
"Doth God know, and is there knowledge in the Most High?" Hath the
Sovereign Ruler forgotten this his great dependency? Surely, he that
is "ALL and always Eye" will not be ignorant of this sad reverse, nor
be unmindful of the lot of Mansoul.

Accordingly, the whole catastrophe is laid open before his all-
searching sight—the fact of the fall, and the agent of the fall. The
whole scene was spread out as a panorama before his eye. He saw
the Tempter, and the tempted, and the force of the temptation. He
heard the lies and falsehoods of the wily DIABOLUS, and observed the
crafty intrigues of the cunning ILL-PAUSE. And it sent a pang of grief
and sorrow through the heart of God when he found the will, and
mind, and affection of Mansoul thus perverted and thus vile; the
town in arms, in open rebellion, garrisoned, strengthened, and
defended against its appointed King.

In open Court.—And what a scene that glorious, grand, august as-
sembly! All heaven intent on earth and its sad story. Angels, that
once sounded forth the praise of a new-created world, now droop their
heads, and fold their wings, and hang their harps upon the willows.
The morning stars that once shouted aloud for joy, now hide themselves for very shame and sorrow; and if ever a tear did stain the
golden pavement, it had been then—when the heart of God himself
was smitten with such a rending stroke of sorrow and of sadness!

God is angry for man's sin, and he is sorrowful, too; but "more in sorrow than in anger." Then did the Father and the Son retire into the mysterious inner chamber of the Divine counsel for consultation as to the means to be employed to save and rescue fallen Man.

And now is the making of the glorious Covenant, by which the eternal Son doth plight his covenanted word, that He Himself would come, and, in his own person, lay the foundation of a yet more glorious kingdom. Not as the Caesars, and other conquerors, who laid the foundation of their thrones in the blood of their enemies; Immanuel proposes to establish his throne by *his own* blood, and thus to effect the soul's perfect deliverance from Satan's power, in which it was previously held in bondage.

The Lord Chief Secretary.—This signifies the Holy Spirit, whose office it is to reveal and make known to man the counsels of the God-head. Of that Spirit doth Christ speak when he saith—"He shall take of mine, and shall show it unto you," John 16:15. The Spirit makes known the terms of the covenant for the redemption of the world—that man has sinned, and must therefore pay the penalty pronounced against the sinner—the penalty of death. Yet doth it grieve God that man should die, and accordingly, in mercy, a way of escape is provided for him. The appointed scheme is this: a substitute is found, not an angel, nor an archangel, but the Son— IMMANUEL. *He* will come, and bear the sin, and endure the penalty, and satisfy the claims of justice, and pay the debt to its last demand. *He* will stand in the stead of Man; will bear the Father's wrath, the full penalty of the curse; and by his death atone for sin.

The Divine word was pledged—the unalterable word that standeth sure when earth and heaven have passed away—that in the fullness of time Christ would come; and in his coming, yea, even in the promise of his coming, and through faith in the promise, souls should be saved. War is accordingly proclaimed—a mortal strife with Satan; and Jesus will prove, by his love, that he can save man, and by his power, that he can destroy the Destroyer.

This good purpose of God is made known to man through the Holy Scriptures—the writings of the Spirit. These are the good tidings, borne from heaven to earth, in return for the evil tidings which had been borne from earth to heaven. These are the great designs of God against the devices of Satan—the great inauguration of the HOLY WAR!

Came to the ears of Diabolus.—Yes, and Satan is astounded. He had expected some interposition, and had led Mansoul to look for some interference on the part of God; but he had never anticipated the Divine intervention in *this* form; that the covenant of grace should be concluded, and Christ's own word and promise, his love and power, pledged to reclaim lost man. The league of God's omnipotence, omniscience, and omnipresence is now allied for the rescue of the sinner; and it behoveth Satan to bethink himself how he may best resist this great design of God in Christ.

Kept from the ears of Mansoul.—Satan knows what was once the weak point of man, by which the first temptation entered—the hearing sense; so he now strengthens this for himself against the King. He knows well what is the influence, for good or evil, of this Ear-gate of man. Temptations ofttimes enter there and gain the heart; and sometimes good is instilled thereat, and the heart is won to righteousness.

Armor for you I have.—Not without weapons of offence and defense does Satan commit his soldiers to the fierce-fought battlefield. And in this description of the armor of Satan is contained a very contrast to the "whole armor of God," as detailed by the Apostle Paul, Ephesians 6:13–18.

1. *My helmet.*—Instead of the "helmet of salvation" is the "helmet of false peace." This helmet, so long as it is worn, cannot be pierced. The arrows of the mighty may graze it, but they cannot enter. It defends the head in the day of battle, but will not defend it in the day of final rout, when, hurled headlong, its very weight will increase the velocity of the flight, and aggravate the depth of the fall of lost and ruined souls.

2. *My breastplate.*—Not "of righteousness," but of iron; forged in the blazing furnace of the pit, and on the sounding anvil of destruction. This is the hard heart of the impenitent sinner—the deadness of the soul, insensibility of conscience, impervious to the influences of love or fear, of mercy or judgment. This is the dead-lock of the soul; the stony heart is the defensive armor of the soldiers of Satan. The man encased in this hard cuirass is proof alike against the promises and the threatenings, the goodness and severity of God.

3. *My sword.*—Not "of the Spirit," but of the "fiery, lying tongue." The Christian's sword is "the Word of God," the word of truth; the sinner's sword is the word of falsehood. The Christian's tongue is touched with a live coal from off the heavenly altar; the sinner's tongue is also a tongue of fire, but one that is "set on fire of hell." "Their tongue is a sharp sword," Psalm 57:4.

4. *My shield.*—Not "of faith," but "of unbelief." Faith quenches the

fiery darts of the wicked one; unbelief quenches the arrows of conviction. This shield restrained the power of Jesus at Capernaum, and restricted the manifestations of his might. Satan's principle is—Grant nothing, believe nothing, admit nothing, question everything; oppose this shield to every dart of conscience, to every promise of Jehovah, to every word that proceedeth out of the mouth of God! The spirit of unbelief in the carnal heart realizes not the power of God's wrath, the greatness of his love, the completeness of his sacrifice, or the perfection of his holiness; and thus are the arrows of the mighty quenched.

5. *A dumb and prayerless spirit.*—This is the heart that never prays, the soul that never supplicates, the spirit that is too proud to bend the knee. Prayer is the completion of the Christian's armor; the bracing atmosphere of the Christian warrior; the oil to keep his armor bright and burnished—"praying always." And so, by contrast, the completion of the sinner's armor is "the dumb and prayerless spirit"—that spirit that encases the heart, and the sympathies of the heart, and the better feelings of the soul, within the granite rock of impenitency and unconcern; the spirit that is dumb before God, owns no wants, asks no blessings, and waits not upon God.

CHAPTER III

SHADDAI'S CAPTAINS—THE SIEGE

OUTLINE OF CHAPTER III.—Shaddai's Four Great Captains—Boanerges, Conviction, Judgment, and Execution.—Their Commission.—Their Ensigns, Colors, and Escutcheons.—The Parley at Ear-gate.—Ill Success.—Ear-gate guarded by Mr. Prejudice and his Deaf-men.—The Assault.—The Watch-word.—Mansoul Resists.—Prisoners Taken.—Alarms and Fears of Mansoul.—The Parley Renewed.—Overtures and Conditions.—Understanding and Conscience disturb the Town, and are imprisoned.

Preparing to send an army.—Throughout the dark picture of the past, there has appeared but one solitary gleam of hope, namely, that SHADDAI had heard of the revolt, and had determined on his own course of counteraction, as embodied in the covenant of his Son. Yet, ere long, even this hope is shaded and darkened by the extraordinary efforts of Satan, building additional strongholds, and making the town stronger and stronger for his own possession. The covenant of Jesus alarms DIABOLUS; he accordingly garrisons the soul for himself, and makes it secure as a prey to his teeth: and now it would seem as though all light and hope had utterly fled. The Understanding is darkened and imprisoned; the Conscience is debauched and depraved; the Will is perverted and enslaved; the whole man is degraded, and, in his degradation, is armed against the King.

Yet, at this point the story turns again, and light once more appears. Heaven hath not forgotten its promise; IMMANUEL hath not been unmindful of his covenant; and now it may be said—"The Lord is a man of war; the Lord is his name," Exodus 15:3.

While Satan has been preparing for resistance, God has been preparing for the assault; and now the preparations are well-nigh completed. Yet, IMMANUEL comes not in his own person, but, as it were, through his representatives—his chosen messengers.

These four Captains.—The Captains of SHADDAI'S army represent the ministers of God's word and will, the preliminary dispensations of

God's covenant, the earlier efforts of Jehovah to win back the Soul of man. First, is the *preaching* of the Word; this is followed up by the *convictions* of the soul; these neglected, the next step is the delivery of *judgment* and sentence; and after this, if the soul be still impenitent, is the *execution* of the sentence.

These Captains are described as being "stout and rough-hewn men;" and so they had need to be—"sons of thunder," laying bare the heart, and by the rough handling of the conscience making themselves felt. Strong, indeed, must be the assault that is to break down the strongholds of Satan; loud as thunder the voice that is to open Ear-gate; bold and demonstrative the array that is to command the attention of Eye-gate; strict, severe, and searching the ministry that is to break open the walls and gates of the Soul against the purpose of the Will, and enter the very Castle of the Heart, and take the whole man captive to IMMANUEL. And, as is the nature and character of the Captains, so are the associations of their office and command.

BOANERGES, with his Ensign, Mr. THUNDER, bearing the "black colors," with the escutcheon of the "three burning bolts," represents an awakening ministry, that speaks not words of peace, but words of warning; able to "reprove, rebuke, exhort;" and, knowing the terrors of the Lord, to "persuade men."

CONVICTION, with his Ensign, Mr. SORROW, bearing the "pale colors," with the escutcheon of the "open Book of the Law," whence issued a flame of fire, represents the law of God, wide open to the gaze, extended to the view; written within and without, and making no secret of its terrors. And with Conviction comes Sorrow—deep, heartfelt compunction, pale with terror—a horrible dread hath overwhelmed him.

JUDGMENT, with his Ensign, Mr. TERROR, bearing the "red colors," with the escutcheon of the "burning fiery furnace," represents the soul self-convicted, self-condemned, in view of the sentence of the law. It was in view of something such as this that Israel did exceedingly fear and quake before the Mount. The "colors" of this dread Captain are "red" with blood—the blood of the slain. Therefore, when Paul reasoned of this "judgment," Felix *trembled*.

EXECUTION, with his Ensign, Mr. JUSTICE, bearing also the "red colors," with the escutcheon of the "fruitless tree, and the axe lying at its root," represents the words of judgment as being no vain or idle words; the thunder of the law not innocent and harmless, as are summer peals. Here are the stern words of Justice, which has been wronged, and means to be avenged. Here are the demands of the drawn Sword, that thirsts for blood, and will not be sheathed until it shall be satisfied.

So they set forward to march.—It was a long and tedious journey, extending over "many days;" for now was MANSOUL far from God. At length they reach the precincts of the town, and set down before Ear-gate—the place of hearing.

Now begins the eloquent description of God's direct dealings with the soul. He will make his Word to be heard, and his judgments to be seen. And such things ofttimes arrest the attention of the soul; and the thoughts and desires, and hopes and fears (the inhabitants of the town), come out to see and to observe. This is sure to provoke the jealousy of Satan. Any heeding of God's Word, any hearkening to God's message, arouses him to keep his goods in peace; and, accordingly, he drives back the awaking thoughts, and the observant feelings and perceptions of the soul, to their refuge and covering of darkness. The part and duty of the allies of Satan within the heart is not to come out, and look, and gaze upon the Divine dealings with the soul, but rather self-defense, yea, and even bold defiance against the King! Therefore does Satan ever chide his servants with unfaithfulness to his dominion when they lend an ear to the message of the Divine Word. He rallies them, and, ere long, wins them back again to hatred of the Word.

"Take-heed-what-you-hear."—This is the name of BOANERGES' trumpeter. The name he bears, the office he wields, and the treatment he received, all combine to teach an instructive lesson. Thrice was this officer sent forth to summon the town; twice did he blow his blast, but there was none to answer. Yet a third time, and the sound is heard, but is answered by proud and angry words.

Here is a description of the parley of Divine grace with the soul, through the ministry of the Word. The Will is first addressed; for without its permission the sound cannot reach the soul. And what a crafty device is that of Satan, in making the Will of man his viceroy, having command of the castle, the walls, and the gates; that is, as the margin interprets it—"the heart, the flesh, and the senses!"

God causes his ministers to sound the Gospel trumpet for audience. God thus "reasons" with man (Isaiah 1:18). Man, in reply, quotes his service and allegiance to another master, and proposes to consult that master's will. But God will not recognize the mastery of Satan, and therefore still continues to address himself to *man*. He ever keeps these twain ideas separate, because they are separable—

Satan and man. He determines to destroy the one, but to save the other.

The Trumpeters sounded.—This is a blast of many trumpets, to call the attention of the town. This would mean some special effort, a season of special preaching of the Word—so oft, so frequent, and so commanding, as that man *must* hear, and God will force himself upon the attention of the soul.

Desired to see the Lord Mayor.—This is the great virtue of the preached Word: it calls up the ruling powers of the soul, for audience. Here, the preaching voice sought to summon the Understanding, once a chief ruler in the heart, but now darkened and imprisoned. Satan has bound the Understanding, and, rather than allow it to speak face to face with the Divine Word, he comes down himself to hold parley with the trumpeter of the King. But, no, this must not be—the Word must still be addressed to the Understanding; and who can tell but that even yet it may hear and understand the message of peace?

What is the reason of all this ado?—This question of DIABOLUS calls forth the fourfold answer of the four great Captains. They take no notice of the giant, but proceed to address their words and exhortations to MANSOUL.

BOANERGES is the first to speak. His terms are, pardon and peace, or else the alternative of force. The message of the "sons of thunder" is a stern, unflinching demand—peace or war. If man will not submit, then God will take the matter into his own all-powerful hands, and win the day by force.

CONVICTION follows up the word. After the Gospel is preached, then follow the results—the convictions of the soul. These open up the plague of one's own heart; convince the man of sin; and expose his rebellion before his eyes. Conviction is the argument of the man with himself; the painful, agonizing soliloquy of the soul; the inward striving of the Spirit of God with the heart of man.

JUDGMENT now speaks; always does speak, if the strivings of conviction have borne no fruit unto repentance. And, as he speaks, he unfurls the blood-red colors of destruction. He lays emphasis upon the fact of man's rebellion, his acts of treason and perfidy against the King. He tells of threatened wrath, treasured up against the day of wrath.

EXECUTION now advances—he the last, most terrible of all; and where he stands, stands also Justice, displaying the escutcheon of his standard—the fruitless tree and the sharp-edged axe! And what admonitory words are these—Thou fruitless bough! the axe is laid *at* thy root, before it is laid *to* thy root! This is a solemn truth for all. Between these two acts—the depositing of the axe *at* the root, and the laying of the axe *to* the root—between these twain is the season of repentance. Is not God long-suffering, ever saying, "Wilt thou turn? or shall I smite?"

Incredulity began, and said.—Man's spirit of Unbelief gives back an answer to the Captains. This was part of MANSOUL'S Diabolonian armor—the Shield of Unbelief. This defense does INCREDULITY now oppose to appeals of the Captains. Unbelief scorns the message, upbraids the messengers, defies their armies, resents their interference, and at length retires from the gate, caring nothing, hoping nothing, believing nothing, fearing nothing!

Seconded by Willbewill.—What Unbelief suggests, the carnal Will is sure to second and support. The whole tone and character of the unbeliever's Will is against the appeals of heaven. He has no wish to be other than he is; and so long as the Will seconds Unbelief, there is no access for good into the soul.

The Recorder also added, etc.—There is much significance in the answer of this power of the unbelieving soul. FORGET-GOOD desires ease and peace and quietude. Forgetfulness is not an *active* agency of the mind; it needs but time and rest to compass the oblivion of that which is good. And this is the ruling power that has taken the place of that active principle called CONSCIENCE. It loves not to be disturbed; for if the Recorder be at rest, the town itself is quiet and at peace. Satan ever seeks to lull the sinner into the unbroken quietude of apathy and unconcern.

Old Mr. Prejudice.—One precaution, however, was taken; and this forms one of the most ingenious of the many able pictures described by Bunyan's pen—Old Mr. PREJUDICE is set for the defense of Ear-gate, with an army of Deaf-men! What a splendid stroke of the great master-mind is this! There is no such effective sentinel of the hearing sense, as Prejudice. It closes many an ear; it occupies many a heart; it checks many an inquiry; it slays many a soul. With Prejudice and his deaf-men, Satan will keep watch and ward for yet many a day, forbidding access to the words of life; and, knowing that "faith cometh by hearing," he will carefully guard and bolt and double-lock the door of Ear-gate against the sound of the Gospel of Christ.

They prepared themselves.—The Captains being thus defeated in their efforts, more severe measures must now be tried. IMMANUEL has sent forth his armies to re-conquer MANSOUL; and it must be done. Accordingly, an assault is made on Ear-gate. The war-cry and watchword is—"Ye must be born again." This was the first watch-word with which the Great Teacher assailed the ears of Nicodemus, and by which he ultimately gained the heart of the Jewish ruler. The sound of this cry is heard in the soul; but it provokes opposi-tion—"shout against shout, and charge against charge." This is the evil and corrupt nature, arguing against the word of God and its demands upon the soul.

High-mind and Heady.—Human pride is one of the most prominent of the elements of opposition to God's designs of mercy. It stands in the way of Divine grace; it owns no need; it acknowledges no sin; it sees no necessity for salvation. Pride resists the overtures of God's grace, and rejects the offers of the Gospel. The assault of the Cap-tains at this time is unsuccessful.

Here is described the determined and continued resistance of the soul. Sermons, appeals, inward convictions, judgments, and the execution of wrath—all are tried in vain. There is, no doubt, much rending, and battering, and breaking up; and the soul is not at peace, but in open war—against the Word, against its own convic-tions, against God's judgments; and yet, against all these, the "Old man" still prevails!

And is not this made good in our own experience? Many a Boa-nerges, with the commission of his King, can effect just nothing toward the dislodgement of Satan. The carnal mind, the sensual principles, the fleshly nature—all are leagued together against the entrance of the Word that giveth light.

Three young fellows.—This introduces an incident of the War. These three young men at first enlisted into the King's army, but were one day taken prisoners. At the suggestion of Satan they changed sides, and thenceforward served in the army of DIABOLUS. These three men represent three earthly principles, which, accord-ing to circumstances, are prepared to serve either master. There are some useful lessons to be derived from this episode of the War. For example:—

1. Mr. TRADITION.—There is no absolute necessity that Tradition should serve the purposes of Satan. "Tradition" means "handing down;" and surely its office might be exercised in the transmission of that which is *good.* Indeed, Tradition was first employed in this service. Once there was no written Word; for many centuries the truth was indebted to Tradition for handing down the Word of God

from generation to generation. But soon did Tradition fall into the rear, and by and by it was taken prisoner by Satan, and pressed into his service; so that, in the day of Christ, men did "make void the law of God through their tradition."

2. Mr. HUMAN-WISDOM.—Once man was wise; and in that day his wisdom was his protection. And Human Wisdom might have continued as a defense of Divine truth upon the earth. Yet this, too, did soon fall into the rear; and, having been taken prisoner, has ever since been under the hand of Satan. The Apostle said in his day, that "the world by wisdom knew not God;" and that "not many wise men after the flesh" had God called. Yea, and even in the present day of light and knowledge, do we not too often find human wisdom and earthly science engaged in the service of Satan, and, through the cunning device of the devil, turned against the truth?

3. Mr. MAN'S-INVENTION.—The inventive capacity of man was once for the promotion of the truth—his thoughts and designs being engaged in the service of God. But this principle also became a coward, and was taken prisoner. "God made man upright; but they have sought out many inventions," Ecclesiastes 7:29. It is man's invention that has brought forth false doctrine, false worship, and errors in faith and practice.

And Captain ANYTHING still survives, to capture fresh prisoners and to conduct new recruits to battle. Under the standard of "indifferentism" more souls are lost than, perhaps, under the more definite systematic forms of error.

Some execution upon the town.—These spiritual conflicts, however, take some effect upon the soul. Unbelief trembles; the more presumptuous sins are abandoned; and carnal pride is leveled in the dust of humiliation. Under the preaching of the Word, the soul of the sinner is ill at ease. The alarms are too loud, intense, and frequent to allow peace to the conscience. The depths are now being stirred, and convictions war within the soul. The flesh and the spirit are in conflict; and God's Spirit now *strives* with man. The thunderings of BOANERGES awaken that "dreadful sound" which so alarmed the Pilgrim in the outset of THE PILGRIM'S PROGRESS. And men would more readily give heed to these oft-repeated messages, were it not for the opposition of Unbelief, and the inconstancy of the Will.

Sent three times.—The preaching of the Word to sinners is as a summons to the soul, calling it to surrender. And these trumpet blasts increase in intensity. First, in words of peace, with promises of pardon, and admonitions to beware. Then, more roughly, with threatenings for their obduracy of spirit in this long delay. And yet again, more roughly still, as though in doubt between the offers of mercy and the execution of judgment.

These oft-repeated calls bring the soul to anxious thought, and to some sense of its miserable state. And, first of all, the purpose is to offer certain overtures. The Will of man would rather have peace than this continual war at its gates. And if peace can be obtained by offering terms, the Will is content to negotiate concessions. The carnal nature, when under these alarms, would serve two masters if it could: that is, let God be King, but let the carnal principles remain; let the power of evil still abide in the soul; let the man still revel in his sensual delights and enjoyments; let no new or better law be binding on the soul. Have we not at times offered these conditions ourselves, when in our secret hearts we have proposed to serve God, provided we may serve Satan too, and indulge the carnal desires of the flesh? Many sinners would agree to recognize SHADDAI as their titular ruler, their nominal lord, on condition that no law of God should have dominion over them.

But this cannot be. New wine must not thus be put into old bottles; the new cloth agreeth not with the old garment; the house must not be built partly on the rock and partly on the sand. "All or none" is the demand of Jesus! Unbelief resents this, and renews the rebellion of the soul against its once-loved King. A bad adviser is this spirit of unbelief in man; it is Satan's trusty servant, that ever seeks to stand between Christ and the soul. When the fears of the awakened sinner urge him to make terms with God, the power of unbelief steps in, driving the soul back again to its iron chains and cruel bondage.

Put Mansoul into a mutiny.—These agitations and commotions of the soul are generally followed by the awaking of the Understanding from its darkness, and the arousing of Conscience from its debauchery. When these powers are thus awakened, they are instantly out in the highways and thoroughfares of the soul, making their protest heard far and near. It is only by darkening the Understanding and debauching the Conscience that these ruling powers in man can be restrained from forcing their testimony upon the soul.

Here the Understanding and Conscience are represented as coming to a knowledge of the doings of Unbelief, and the overtures of the carnal Will. The enlightened understanding and the awakened conscience are always on the side of truth; they ignore the proposals of the carnal mind as utterly unworthy the acceptance of Jehovah, and protest against man's spirit of unbelief when it takes upon itself to act as spokesman for the soul. Hence arises a war of words; strife and fierce contention rage within; there is a mutiny in Mansoul; Unbelief is assailed even in his own dwelling place; and now a crisis is at hand!

This is a glowing description of the soul's unrest when under the protest of an awakened conscience. The rabble of man's thoughts and fears take sides, and the multitude is divided. Some take the side of Conscience, and others rally around the standard of Unbelief. Some cry one thing, and some another. The soul is, meanwhile, tossed with tempests; as when fierce storms blow upon the deep, and the craft is driven to and fro upon the wave. And, by-and-by, from words they proceed to blows; and not only do the thoughts accuse one another, but they come into actual contact and collision.

Bunyan depicts, at this stage, a well-drawn portrait of the soul under conviction of sin, and yet under the bondage of Satan. Resistance is tried, until it can resist no longer. Then it makes overtures, and proposes half measures. These are rejected. Unbelief then rises up, and once more rallies the soul to take a decided stand *against* the King. The alarm of the soul will not admit of this. Meanwhile, the Understanding and Conscience have broken loose, and mightily disturb the soul. A desperate conflict ensues—thought against thought; hope against fear; deep calleth unto deep; and now is Mansoul brought to that state of disquietude described by the prophet—"The wicked are like the troubled sea, when it cannot rest, whose waters cast up mire and dirt," Isaiah 57:20.

In this conflict of warring elements in the soul, much damage is done to the evil nature. For example:—Rashness is destroyed, and the soul becomes more considerate of its own welfare; Prejudice, once so potent for evil, is trampled under foot; the spirit of Indifference receives rough handling; and the Will, lately so decided, now stands in doubt.

When the uproar was over.—All conflicts must some time cease; the fiercest tempests brawl themselves to rest. And, even so, the convictions of the soul exhaust themselves. This is Satan's opportunity, when he takes advantage of the reaction, and once more imprisons the Conscience and the Understanding. So long as these powers are aroused, there is danger to Satan's kingdom, and Mansoul cannot settle down in peace amid its sins and its corruptions, but must give heed to the protests of the monitor within. The great design of Satan, therefore, is to gain possession of these powers. His tenure of the soul depends upon his dominion over *them*. Accordingly, he now places them once more under arrest—to darken the one, and to debauch the other.

Meanwhile, a trumpeter is sent with another summons to the town. He lays stress upon the power and mightiness of SHADDAI, and that it is not for his weakness, but for his mercy, he thus entreats the soul to be reconciled unto God. This appeal is answered by DIABOLUS, who once more rallies the agitated citizens, and again turns the soul against the offers of mercy. Thus the soul is again enslaved; yea, with a bondage greater than before.

CHAPTER IV

IMMANUEL'S ARMY—THE ASSAULT

OUTLINE OF CHAPTER IV.—The Besiegers appeal to Shaddai.—
Christ the Mediator and Intercessor.—Immanuel must come and
conquer.—The Prince sets forth.—His Five Captains.—Their
Standard-bearers and Escutcheons.—Mansoul beleaguered.—
Mount Gracious and Mount Justice.—The White Flag of Mercy.—
The Red Flag of Judgment.—The Black Flag of Defiance.—Diabolus
speaks through Mouth-gate.—Immanuel answers through Ear-
gate.—His Claim to Mansoul.—The Assault renewed.—Overtures
by Mr. Loth-to-Stoop.—Rejected by Immanuel.—Ear-gate assaulted
and shaken.—Eye-gate assailed and broken open.—Overtures of
Diabolus again rejected.

So they ceased that way.—In the main the assault had been unsuccessful. Owing to the influence of the ruling powers of the soul,
Satan retained his dominion. Yet much and serious damage had
been done to the carnal nature—its pride had been humbled, and its
more flagrant and presumptuous sins had been abandoned; but still
Mansoul was not taken, and the four Captains, accordingly, retire
for a season, and meanwhile hold a council of war. They resolve
upon two plans: (1) to keep the town still in a state of continual
alarm; and (2) to forward a petition to the King, their great Master,
SHADDAI.

Here it would be well to keep in mind the double interpretation
of this part of the Allegory: (1) the *general* interpretation, as it refers
to the dispensation of the Law, with its thunders and convictions,
seeking to recover the soul to God; and (2) the *particular* interpretation, as it refers to the strivings of Divine grace with the soul of the
sinner, through the preliminary ministrations of the Word.

A petition should be drawn up.—This was an important step on the
part of SHADDAI'S Captains. They seek back to him who had sent
them, and ask fresh counsel and instructions at his hands. The
petition sets forth that they had done as they were commanded;
that they had met with but little success, and as yet the town was

not taken; that Mansoul had been alarmed and terrified, but was as yet *not saved*; and they ask for fresh supports, and for one to lead them who will be greater and stronger than the four great Captains.

This petition means Prayer. It is the Law, "wherein it was weak," acknowledging its ill success, and appealing for a fresh effort from heaven to save the soul. It is also the Ministry of the Word acknowledging its own inefficiency—that of itself it cannot save the soul. Boanerges may preach, Conviction may alarm, Judgment may terrify, and Execution may lay the axe to the root of the tree; but it is only God in Christ who can effectually save the soul.

Mr. Love-to-Mansoul.—The petition is Prayer; and the person who bears the petition indicates the *spirit* of prayer. Here the prayer is winged on the arrow of Love—love to the soul of the sinner. Thus borne to heaven, it soon reaches its destination, and falls into the hands of the King's own Son, IMMANUEL.

So he took it.—Here is a beautiful description of the mediatorial office of Christ, and how he fulfils it. He intercedes for man, and gains what he asks for. Christ receives our prayers—the prayers of faith. He amends them, strengthens them, speaks in their behalf, and presents them to his Father, not as *our* petitions, but *as his own request*. It is this that imparts power to prayer; it is not so much in him that *prays*, as in Him that *intercedes*. We have power with Christ, through faith, because he is our Brother; and Christ has power with God, because He is his Son. Christ accepts our prayers, with their many faults—sometimes asking the wrong things; sometimes asking in the wrong way. But if the heart go with it, then the spirit prays; and the Great High Priest receives the petition upon the golden censer, and presents it for us, and in his own name, before his Father.

In all ministerial work, prayer constitutes an essential element. We may bring the slings and batteries of the Word to bear upon the soul; we may assail Ear-gate, or attract Eye-gate, or touch Feel-gate, or even make an impression on Heart-castle; but all must be in vain, unless Christ shall come himself to save the soul. That only is a living and saving ministry—

> "Where only Christ is heard to speak,
> And Jesus reigns alone."*

And now is the time for the Covenant of IMMANUEL; now will he come himself to perform the work of deliverance. The Father suggests

---

*Charles Wesley, *O for a Heart to Praise My God*, 1742.

this Covenant; the Son accepts its stern conditions, and voluntarily offers himself as the Leader of the host for the salvation of the soul—"Behold, I come!"

How ready were the high ones.—The new covenant of IMMANUEL is ever described in Holy Scripture as a subject of joy and gladness among the Intelligences of heaven. All the great dealings of God with man seem to have commanded the interest of the "high ones" of his glory. When the work of creation was accomplished, it is said that "the morning stars sang together, and all the sons of God shouted for joy," Job 38:7. Again, when the greater work—Redemption—was begun in the birth of Jesus Christ, angels sang the glad tidings over the pasture-plains of Bethlehem, Luke 2:9, 13. And, yet again, when the effect of that redemption is applied to the heart of the poor repentant sinner, it is said, "There is joy in the presence of the angels of God over one sinner that repenteth," Luke 15:10.

Angels are, however, described as evidencing a lively anxiety, amounting even to a feeling of curiosity, as to the great Covenant of God in Christ. Hence the form and gesture of the cherubim over the mercy-seat, lowly bending over the ark, as though inquiring into its inner mysteries, to which allusion is made by the Apostle St. Peter—"Which things the angels desire to look into," 1 Peter 1:12. Again and again did angels intervene as messengers of God to men, conveying tidings, ratifying covenants, and otherwise making known God's mind, and will, and purpose.

And even now angels would gladly be engaged in the work of man's salvation. They would feel it their highest honor to be privileged to do God's work upon earth. But God has preferred laying that honor upon *man*, that by our hands, and not by the hands of angels, his glorious Covenant may be made good. The glad tidings that angels would gladly proclaim, it is our high privilege to make known. How gladly would they fly through all the earth, and blow the Gospel trumpet, and proclaim the acceptable year of the Lord! But God has reserved this work for his own dear Son, and for us who would be "workers together with Christ Jesus."

He addressed himself for his march.—"The Captain of our salvation" now sets forth, but not alone. He comes with ten thousands at his feet, and with his five brave Captains. This expedition is suggestive in all its parts, and includes, within the compass of the description, the whole plan of salvation as revealed and wrought out in Christ.

1. The first is Captain CREDENCE (of whom more by-and-by). He

and his attendants represent Faith, as opposed to INCREDULITY, who reigns within; and this believing Faith is supported by the Promis-es, all of which are guaranteed by blood (the red colors)—the blood of the "Holy Lamb;" and protected by the golden shield—"the shield of Faith." Without Faith Christ cannot be received into the soul.

2. Captain GOOD-HOPE, whose colors are clear as the blue sky, and studded with the brilliant stars of expectation. Though it may be dark, yet there is evidence of sunshine somewhere beyond; and this Hope is "the anchor of the soul."

3. Captain CHARITY, whose colors are green as the springing grass, indicating that holy and abiding Love—to God and man—which causes the fruits of faith to abound in all good works, clasping the otherwise naked and defenseless orphans to its genial and loving bosom.

Thus are the three Graces of the Gospel—Faith, Hope, and Char-ity—here represented as the three mighty Captains of IMMANUEL'S army, with ten thousand men (that is, good thoughts, good hopes, good words, good works) at their command.

4. Captain INNOCENT represents a further characteristic of Christ and of his people. "Harmless as doves" is part of the Christian character, as indicated on the escutcheon and virgin-white colors of this brave Captain.

5. Captain PATIENCE is that spirit of the Master, that is long-suffering of evil and patient in tribulation. However dark or black the prospect (the black colors), the true Christian will be enduring of the strife and patient of the conflict. This is just such a Captain as would be worthy of so hard-fought a battlefield.

These are "the things that accompany salvation"—the gifts and graces of the Spirit—Faith in the person of Christ the Savior; Hope in the glorious promises of his word; Charity, that true love to God and to his people; Innocence, in native purity and virtue unadorned; and Patience, that enduring virtue of the true Christian. With these, accompanied by these, encompassed by these, the Great Captain sets forth upon his glorious enterprise.

Battering-rams and slings.—Bunyan represents these to mean the Books of Holy Scripture, constituting a military train that is "mighty, through God, to the pulling down of strongholds."

They environed it.—The town is beleaguered now. When Christ lays siege to the soul, he surrounds it on all sides, and leaves no opening for escape. He is in earnest, and he means to conquer; and however man may resist, yet Christ will overcome at last. Therefore he environs both walls and gates, and lays siege round about the flesh, and the senses, and the heart of man.

The White Flag.—And now commence the dispensations of God in his dealings with the soul. He begins with Mercy. Justice makes the first demands; but Mercy makes the first advance. Man is advertised, by the White Flag, that IMMANUEL is even yet minded to deliver the soul, if the soul *will* but be delivered. If this offer be accepted, all is well; but if it be rejected, it will but increase the sinner's condemnation.

The Red Flag.—And Mansoul *did* reject the offer. The flag of truce, and peace, and mercy was exposed in vain. So now the Red Flag of judgment is unfurled from Mount Justice. Yet even by this terrible sight they were unmoved. Even the sight of the "three golden doves" had not sufficed to win them; and now the sight of the "burning fiery furnace" does not terrify them. They heeded not this sign.

The Black Flag.—And now the "three burning bolts" are exposed to view. But Mansoul takes no heed to the calls of either Mercy, Judgment, or Execution. And yet IMMANUEL hesitates to fulfill the demands of Justice. The thunder-bolt is balanced, but it is not launched. Mercy still holds back the red hand of Judgment, and still entreats the town—"Be ye reconciled to God." But in vain; for Mansoul answers with a refusal of surrender.

Indeed, so deep has the soul, in this stage of its degradation, sunk in the arms of the Wicked One, that the messengers of the Prince are referred to DIABOLUS for answer. And now Satan himself speaks through Mouth-gate to IMMANUEL. See him cringing to the "stronger than he;" and hear him speak his wily words in his own peculiar language.

He owns IMMANUEL to be God and Lord—SHADDAI'S great, all-powerful Son. He acknowledges, as in the day of Christ, IMMANUEL'S power to torment him, and to cast him out. He seeks to establish his claim to Mansoul on the double plea: (1) of lawful conquest and (2) of its own accord and willingness to serve him. This latter is the powerful plea that man has put in the mouth of Satan—that by man's own vote and universal will he is enthroned as the "god of this world."

Immanuel stood up and spake.—Not without challenge does Satan propound his claims to Mansoul. Accordingly, IMMANUEL answers him—Not in open field has Satan won the soul, but by craft and cunning, by lies and horrible hypocrisies. He belied God; he promised, and did not perform; he cast down the image, and erased the superscription, of Jehovah. Therefore, at his hands will he require it, and upon his head will he visit the wrong.

And, moreover, in counter-claim, IMMANUEL pleads his right still to the ownership of Mansoul: 1. By creation; his Father built and fashioned it. 2. By inheritance; he is his Father's only Son, and therefore the heir of all things. 3. By donation; all is made over to him by gift, which cannot be revoked. 4. By purchase; even by the ransom of his blood, as the surety for Mansoul under the Covenant of his Father. 5. Not by half-measures, but wholly and fully; in granting the request of mercy, his Father's law and justice were well satisfied. And, 6. He has come forth by commandment of his Father to deliver Mansoul; yea, and he *will* deliver it!

And now he speaks a word to Mansoul—a word of warning, and yet also a winning word. He yearns over the prostrate sinner; brings his sin to his remembrance; pities and commiserates his desperate condition; and yet he hesitates, as though still in doubt—"What shall I do unto thee? Shall I fall upon thee, and grind thee to powder, or make thee a monument of the richest grace?" The Prince inclines to mercy. The axe is *at* the root; not yet is it laid *to* the root.

Thus does Jesus rebuke the Tempter; and thus does he in turn speak counsel to the soul. Alas! how often does he speak to deaf ears and to deaf hearts, to men uncircumcised in heart and ears! He speaks, he pleads, he numbers up his claims, and urges them upon the soul; but all in vain. He offers mercy, and we accept it not; he threatens judgment, and we heed it not; he hurls defiance, and we abide unmoved. Having eyes, we see not; having ears, we hear not; and having hearts, we do not understand!

Calls his army together.—IMMANUEL now determines upon more vigorous measures. He summons his army in array—captains, colors, escutcheons, ensigns, battering-rams, slings, and soldiers—for an assault. When all these are brought to bear upon the soul, the aspect of affairs is sufficiently alarming; and DIABOLUS *is* alarmed by reason of this vast array that is displayed against him.

Resolved upon certain propositions.—DIABOLUS now determines to attempt the fortune of another overture of conditions. He sends the petition by the hands of a Diabolonian agent, Mr. LOTH-TO-STOOP. This is not prayer, but presumption; nor does it emanate from the soul, but from Satan. The name of the messenger indicates the spirit that prompts the overture, even the pride of the carnal nature, which will not stoop to the yoke of Jesus, or submit itself to the sovereignty of the rightful King.

Now, observe the gradation of the overtures of Satan, from his maximum offer down to his lowest demand—

1. He offers to give up half the soul, and would retain the other half. "They profess that they know God; but in works they deny him," Titus 1:16. This half allegiance is instantly rejected. "All is mine!" saith the Prince.

2. Let IMMANUEL be the nominal and tituler ruler of all; only reserve a portion for the dominion of DIABOLUS. Thus men cry, "Lord, Lord," but their hearts are far from God. "Really, not nominally—all or none!" saith the Prince.

3. Only assign a private dwelling for Satan in the soul; and all the rest is thine! No, there shall be left not even a corner in the heart of man for Satan—"All is mine!" repeats the Prince.

4. Then, have it all; only let Satan, as a wayfaring man, tarry at times within the soul. Nay, not even this; 'tis perilous to the soul!

5. May permission, then, be granted to his friends to trade with the town? No, nor this; no trade or traffic with Diabolonians! If any such be found, they shall lose land, and liberty, and life.

6. Yea, even the occasion of letters and other opportunities must be denied him; for even these would tend to keep up the alienation and estrangement of the soul.

7. Not even a token, keepsake, or memento of the past shall be permitted: these tend to refresh the carnal memory, and to revive the affection toward the former sins. Not a shred must be left behind.

8. The last and least of the overtures asks permission for occasional visits, on special emergencies; and this, too, is denied. On no account, and on no possible pretext, can IMMANUEL agree to give room to Satan in the soul. Extermination, root and branch, is the purpose of the Prince.

Such are the overtures of Satan in the soul—from higher demands to lower, and thence to the lowest. He would hold dominion on any terms. Any link of connection, any bond of union, any opportunity of intercourse, any door of access would satisfy him; only let him have a hold on the soul of man. These overtures rejected, Satan refuses to surrender possession of the soul.

I must try the power of my sword.—Once more to the assault! The preaching of the Word is once again commissioned to go forth, followed by the conviction of the soul. In this assault Captain CONVICTION is sorely wounded. We ofttimes trifle with our convictions, and sometimes fight against them, and at times even wound them. These dread conflicts, however, work more grievous damage to DIABOLUS; for we find that, on the occasion of this assault, the spirit of proud boasting ceases; and the fancied security of the soul is utterly put out of the way by the strong conflict of conviction; the feelings, too, cease to be the measure of spiritual experience; and a whole host of Diabolonian and carnal influences are put to flight.

Yet, for all this, the soul is not taken. These sore conflicts and opposing convictions must be again and again repeated, ere the surrender of the soul to Christ. Meanwhile, the offers of mercy are once more spread forth before the town. These free offers of grace, thus often exhibited to the soul, render Satan uneasy in his habitation; and now, fearing for the issue, he ventures upon another series of overtures. In doing so he assumes somewhat of the character of an angel of light; and suggests, as the carnal nature sometimes does, moral reformation, rather than spiritual regeneration, to the awakened sinner.

The soul is now brought to this state, that it proposes to lay down all open and violent opposition to Christ; to examine itself, and know its transgression and sin; to give attention to the external means of grace; and promote a general reformation of life. But, with all these, Satan is not cast out. This is the cunning compromise of the crafty serpent. He would have the man to know the theory of religion, to attend the means of grace, to subscribe to religious enterprises; but he will also be himself within the man all the time. Well did IMMANUEL respond—"Oh, full of deceit!"

If Satan cannot urge his victim on through all the dregs of open ungodliness; if the conviction of the soul, and the alarm of conscience, are so strong as to deter the sinner from leading an openly profane life, the great enemy of souls is prepared to accept lower terms of occupation. He can become a fair-spoken moralist and teacher, and if he can only induce the soul to rest upon its own works for salvation, he knows that soul is lost, for want of the great salvation.

It is at such a crisis as this that the inward conflict grows fiercer, and more and more intense. Satan, foreseeing the end, and knowing that his time is short, is minded, through malice, to do all possible mischief to the soul. Yes, he will not spare. He enters the heart as a seeming friend, but leaves it as a veritable foe.

And now the troops are set in battle-array for the final assault. Here IMMANUEL imposes one strict command—that a distinction be made between the natives and the Diabolonians. With the old inhabitants—the original nature of man—his soldiers are to deal gently, and to slay not one; but to the Diabolonian crew no quarter is to be shown.

CHAPTER V

THE CAPTURE AND ITS CONSEQUENCES

OUTLINE OF CHAPTER V.—The Assault.—The Watchword.—The Gates shattered.—Conscience seized.—Immanuel marches on.—Diabolus retreats into the Castle (the Heart).—Immanuel enters Mansoul.—Diabolus bound, led captive, and driven out.—The Mansoulians imprisoned.—The Petition of the Prisoners.—To Mr. Would-live, Immanuel returns no answer.—To Mr. Desires-Awake, he will "consider the request."—By Mr. Wet-Eyes, summons the Prisoners.—Hopes and Fears.—Mansoul humbles itself.—Confesses its Rebellion and Sin.—The Token of Pardon and Acceptance.—Proclamation by the Recorder.—Captain Credence enters the Castle.—Good Tidings of Great Joy.

Ear-gate was broken open.—When the Spirit has been long striving with man, through the agency of an awakening ministry, it happens that, ere long, the ears hear and hearken to the sound of the Word preached. The Gospel message enters, and, so far, Christ has gained advantage. He now stands *at* the gate, not yet *within;* and this, too, is only the outer gate—the hearing of the ears. The main object is the Castle. To gain the *Heart* is the ultimate aim of IMMANUEL. Till his standard floats from the centre of the town, the great object is unachieved. There DIABOLUS reigns; and from that throne he must be dislodged.

To this intent the slings are played—the Word, with its threaten-ings, is brought to bear upon the outward ears—the golden slings, with the arrows of the Lord, tipped with the love of Christ, first to wound, and then to heal.

The street was straight.—A highway and thoroughfare leads straight up from the ear to the conscience; and the conscience of man is an outwork of the heart. The way from the ear to the heart lies through the conscience, which is accordingly now assailed. A troubled con-science ofttimes follows after the admonitions of a powerful ministry. So now, blow after blow is repeated; the convictions of the soul gather round the conscience; and the judgments of the Lord demand the surrender of the heart to God. By-and-by, the conscience yields, and opens its gates to the ministrations and convictions of the Word. Oh, what it is to feel the conscience awakened by the convictions of sin! Christ so near, thundering at the doors of the heart, and the soul contemplating the terrors of the Lord with a troubled mind!

Execution was busy in other parts.—Execution is the searcher of the soul, the "discerner of the thoughts and intents of the heart," Hebrews 4:12. This principle of the Divine operation searches out the hidden thoughts, the lurking desires—the underground population of Mansoul. By it the Will is brought into subjection, bending its stubborn neck to the yoke of IMMANUEL. And while Execution thus visits the soul, many of the Diabolonian principles are slain; though many still survive, and linger in the carnal nature.

During this season of alarm, the Conscience, the Understanding, and other principles fear for their very lives. All is dread, and death, and darkness—the thundering of battering rams, the slinging of stones, the beating in of the doors of the heart, the storming of the strongholds of Satan, the discovery of lurking sins, and the slaying of the powers of hell in Mansoul.

Agree to draw up a petition.—Of Mansoul it may now be said, "Behold; he prayeth." To this the Prince returned no answer. He had already offered mercy, but the offer had been rejected; and now the soul must learn, through the painful ordeal of hard experience, what it is to offend the majesty of Heaven, and to despise the proffered mercy of IMMANUEL. This prayer brings back no answer of peace, because DIABOLUS is still in possession of the Castle—the Heart. While IMMANUEL is only *at* the gate, and is still refused admission, prayer is but an empty sound. Confession of sin, and expression of sorrow, is but of little worth, while Satan is harbored and treasured in the heart. There may be alarms and fears, and these may drive the soul to penitence and prayer; but there is no answer of peace until the heart is willing to open to the Lord.

Yet is prayer a sign of yielding and submission: and accordingly, while Mansoul prays, the assault is pressed with renewed vigor; the gate is broken open; the warfare (this phase of it) is ended; and Mansoul now awaits the issue.

Then the Prince arose.—Jesus now enters the soul; but not as he would have entered, had the soul submitted to the first offers of mercy. He now enters, as a conqueror, into a subjugated province—upon his own terms and conditions. Jesus enters the walls and gates, and passes through the multitude of the thoughts; and all is uncertainty as to what may be the purport of his silence and reserve, whether it be for death or for life.

Here is the convicted soul on the approach of Jesus; whether it be in wrath or mercy, it knows not. The soul is humbled in the dust; thought answers to thought, and fear to fear. Meanwhile the glorious pomp of the Conqueror fills all the soul with his mighty presence.

Diabolus bound with chains.—And first the great usurper must be utterly cast out. Well might Diabolus have said, as "the stronger than he" now enters the soul, "Surely the bitterness of death is past!" And yet a severer doom, the second death, awaits him. Meanwhile, he is bound hand and foot in chains of darkness; he is stripped of his armor, in which he trusted; he is dragged at the chariot-wheels of the Conqueror; and forth in the sight of Eye-gate is he driven, a spectacle to angels and to men. The eyes of the soul beheld that sight—the casting out of the destroyer. The soul was relieved that day of a weary burden. The cause of sin, the power of sin, the love of sin—all cast down at one blow. Great was the triumph of Immanuel. *Amen and Amen*

Terror and dread.—Yet the *sin* of Mansoul still remained—the conscience of sin, and the guilt of sin; all the terrible past is yet to be avenged. The soul's rebellion, mutiny, disobedience, must all be accounted for; and now the reckoning time has come. Jesus has entered as a Conqueror, but he does not yet abide in the soul as a Savior. Mansoul had refused mercy when it was offered; and now it must needs pass through a process—a painful process—of conviction, and sorrow, and deep regret, and of weary suspense as to what the end may be. For, though Satan has been cast out, there is yet enough of sin in Mansoul to sink it into a thousand deeps. Not yet has dawned her day of liberty.

The process begins by the imprisonment of the Will, the Understanding, and the Conscience. These were once the ruling powers of Mansoul. It was in their power to sway the town for good or evil; this power they lent to Satan; and now, at the order of the Prince, they are in prison, and cannot get forth. Such is the dread suspense of the troubled soul, that has trifled with its day of grace. Its spiritual state is low and depressed—"Out of the depths have I cried unto thee, O Lord." It is in doubt, darkness, uncertainty, and misery, under a consciousness of judgment provoked, and of wrath deserved. This is the hard discipline of the soul, while it is caused to pass through a great fight of affliction, ere it receives peace and pardon, and enjoys the blessedness of an indwelling Christ.

By the hand of Mr. Would-Live.—Now Mansoul prays; and the spirit of the prayer is indicated by the name of the messenger that bears the petition—Mr. WOULD-LIVE. This is the lowermost grade of prayerful motive. It simply *seeks for life,* and asks that judgment maybe stayed. It is the first message of convinced and awakened souls— "Spare us, good Lord!" Even the ungodly would rather live than die. To this petition no answer is returned; it is received, but in silence; and all is fear in Mansoul.

Mr. Desires-Awake.—This is a higher grade of spiritual experience. The soul is now conscious of its deep slumber, wrapped in the coverlet of night and darkness. It is high time to awake out of sleep; and it now desires to awake. Here is a picture worthy of a pencil dipped in living light: the prostrate messenger—no pride, but all abasement, in lowly reverence before the throne. This is the penitential spirit of prayer that moves IMMANUEL; and accordingly, touched by the prayer of the penitent, prostrate, and humbled soul, "Jesus wept," and gives the promise that "he will consider of the request." *Mercy O Lord ?*

Meanwhile, the whole soul is filled with anxiety, and in a spirit of expectancy awaits the return of the messenger. The prayerful soul always expects and awaits an answer. The tidings of future consideration of the prayer is capable of an adverse or favorable interpretation, as hope or fear is the interpreter to the soul. On this occasion hopes and fears were once more in contact and collision. It is always so with the convinced soul, when the Spirit is striving with man, and the arrows of conviction are rankling in the conscience. The soul, under these circumstances, knows not what to think; it is under a heavy load of sorrow, sin, and shame; it is deeply exercised in penitential prayer; and prays, and prays, and yet receives no answer of peace. Conscience is troubled, and communicates its doubts and fears to the whole man; and this is the beginning of a great change.

A third Petition.—Mansoul is learning the great lesson, that "men ought always to pray, and not to faint." So far, there has been but little encouragement shown in answer to prayer; and yet the soul prays on. This time the prayer consists of a lowly confession of sin, and an earnest appeal to mercy.

Mr. Good-Deed.—Ultimate success depends upon the spirit in which this prayer shall be presented; and ill-success had well nigh attended it, owing to the proposition to send the petition by one whose name was GOOD-DEED. This is designed to represent the soul resting upon its own merit and self-sufficiency, and in this spirit presenting itself as a suppliant. Well was it for the soul that this proposition was rejected; for when the sinner seeks for mercy, "boasting is excluded," Romans 3:27.

Mr. Wet-Eyes.—In these delineations of "the spirit of prayer," Bunyan displays a marvelous insight into the spirit of man, in his progressive stages of alarm, conviction, and repentance. Here is a beautiful and striking description of the soul in an advanced state of spiritual awakening. Poor in spirit, humbled in the dust, suffused with tears, wholly distrustful of self, and yet able to "speak well to a petition;" crying for mercy, life, pardon, and peace.

The prayer that reaches highest is that which rises from the lowest depth of humiliation. The arrow that speeds the farthest is that which is winged from the greatest bending of the bow. The nearest point to the throne is the footstool. And so this "poor man, and of a broken spirit," is permitted the privilege of nearest access to the Prince, and receives the warmest welcome at his hands. The petition, as presented by him, was characterized by the very deepest prostration of spirit, and by true humility of soul. Prayer thus offered, in the spirit of repentance, in lowly reverence, and in godly fear, is sure to attract the attention of IMMANUEL, who answers the praying but imprisoned soul—"I will consider your petition, and will answer it so as will be for my glory." Amen Lord ♡

Bring the prisoners out to me.—The imprisoned soul is not immediately delivered; it must be made to feel how dreadful a thing it is to sin against the Lord. Mansoul has been taken in open rebellion, in the impiety of its sin; it has been alarmed by the terrible Captains, and also by the multitude of its own thoughts and fears. And now the summons to the prisoners to come forth and present themselves before the offended Prince renews all their worst and most gloomy anticipations. Conscience is afraid to meet the Lord; the Understanding and the Will know their own guilt and vileness, and fear to face the Judge. The thoughts of the soul are guilty; its fears are fresh; its hopes are low.

In execution of this summons to the soul, the preached Word and the Convictions that follow the same are represented as conducting the imprisoned soul to Christ; while the Judgment of God and the Execution of his law are left within the heart, searching out the thoughts and trying the reins, keeping watch and ward over the rising feelings of the soul, and utterly humbling the spirit of human pride. Such are the strivings of the Spirit with the soul, when the Lord's arm is bared and stretched forth, when his Word is quick and powerful, and the soul agonizing in the pain and travail of the new birth.

The prisoners went down.—The procession of the convicted soul to Christ is with BOANERGES going before, and CONVICTION following after. Here is honor laid upon the Word of God, conducting men to Christ by its summons to the Understanding and the Conscience, while Conviction follows, constraining the Will of man. The Word *leads*, while Conviction *drives* the soul to the place where Jesus is. So that men come to Christ, led by the awakening Word, and are driven by the convictions of the heart. At such a time the soul is bound in chains of guilt; clad in the mourning garb of deep repentance; with the evidence of self-condemnation, as a rope around its neck; and crying out for mercy, where it expects only to meet with judgment and wrath—"Be merciful to me, a sinner!"

They covered their faces with shame.—This is that godly sorrow that worketh repentance. It dares not even to look up. The contrast is felt, in all its magnitude, between their sin and Christ's holiness, between his glory and their degradation. This is the inevitable result of a near approach to Jesus: apart from Christ we may possibly glory in our own righteousness; but in his holy presence we feel our own shame and confusion of face.

At this point of the Allegory occurs that striking colloquy, or examination, that illustrates the dealings of God with the truly penitent sinner. By a series of questions, Jesus conducts the soul, as through a refining process, to that open confession of its sin, and that hearty repentance, that finds its level in the dust. A full and unreserved expression of past sin, rebellion, and disobedience, is thus elicited. The soul accuses itself, and names its own deserved punishment—"Death, Lord, and the deep!"

A perfect conquest and victory.—Jesus is the conqueror. He has prevailed by love; and now he proclaims both pardon and peace to the soul. DIABOLUS is overcome; Mansoul is free; and there is joy in heaven over this sinner that repenteth; only, as yet the evidence of this great change was wanting to the soul. The grant of pardon is known in heaven, before it is known on earth, or evidenced to the soul. Not so soon do the troubled waters rest. After pardon, man needs assurance of the fact; and, for this, Conscience is commissioned to return to the soul, and there to repeat the tidings of the King. Thus is Conscience God's witness to man.

And not without evidence is Conscience thus commissioned. There is the witness of the Spirit, too, bearing witness with our

spirit. There is the parchment roll with its seven seals—the creden-
tial of the soul. There is the change of raiment—fair and glorious
garments; and, instead of ropes—the mark of condemnation—are
chains of gold, showing that "there is now no condemnation." The
soul is free, and with tears of joy, and songs of gratitude, it proceeds
to exercise itself in the inward evidence of pardon and assurance.

Credence to march in at Eye-gate.—We have now seen the old Recorder, CONSCIENCE, restored to his former office. Once more he is free
to speak his mind in the hearing of the soul; and with what alacrity
does he resume his former post! He rings his bell right merrily, and
calls the whole man to audience, and makes the full and open
declaration of the Prince's pardon. Does Conscience thus speak to
us? Have we had the witness within ourselves that God has, for
Christ's sake, freely and fully forgiven all our sin? The deed of
pardon is no secret to the soul, for Conscience is the bearer of the
tidings of the gift.

And when Conscience thus acquaints the soul with the message
of the King, then *Faith* enters the heart. In that very place where
DIABOLUS had set up his polluted reign, and established his unholy
throne, and affixed the filthy and profane writings of the carnal
sense—*there* Faith is now enshrined; thither Faith has entered as
the precursor of the Prince, the forerunner of IMMANUEL. Amen O Lord

And when Faith (CREDENCE) enters the heart, then is the soul also
delivered from the terror of the first four Captains. So long as the
preaching of the Word alarms, and convictions terrify, these principles are as an army of occupation, treading down the soul. Until the
Word brings comfort, BOANERGES will continue to be "a son of *thunder*,"
and so long as Judgment and Execution abide in the heart there can
be no peace. But when Faith enters, all is well; and after Faith next
comes Christ himself. O my Lord

Meanwhile, Mansoul is made acquainted with the gift of pardon;
the whole soul, with all its inhabitants,—its thoughts, hopes,
fears,—is apprised of the great change, and patiently waits for the
Lord's time, when he shall visit her, and dwell in her midst.

Bunyan's description of the joy of Mansoul is significant of many
blessed thoughts: he says, "the townsmen leaped upon the walls for
joy;" and interprets this, in a side-note, to mean that "they tread
upon the flesh." He also says that "the bells did ring," and shows
that by "the bells" he means "lively and warm thoughts" in the soul.

And in that day Faith manifests itself; Captain CREDENCE shows
himself upon the castle heights, so that both Mansoul and IMMANUEL

may see and know his indwelling in the soul; as a side-note again says, "Faith will not be silent, when Mansoul is saved." Accordingly, Faith manifests itself to the eye of the soul and to the all-seeing Eye of the Prince!

CHAPTER VI

ENTRY OF THE PRINCE

OUTLINE OF CHAPTER VI.—Spiritual Exercise and Discipline of the Soul.—The Invitation—"We have room for Thee."—Unreserved Conditions and Unrestricted Sway.—Royal Condescension.—Captain Credence conducts the Prince.—Popular Acclamation and Welcome—"Behold, thy King cometh!"—Immanuel abides in Mansoul.—Immanuel's Captains quartered in the Town.—Visits of the Prince.—High Festivals.—The Town New-modeled.—The Strongholds of Diabolus Destroyed.

Oh, that the Prince would dwell in Mansoul!—Faith has entered the heart, and after Faith comes Christ. Faith is the receptive and the perceptive power of the soul. It is the *eye* of the soul—that sees Jesus; the *ear* of the soul—that hears his Word; the *hand* of the soul—that lays hold on Jesus; the *understanding* of the heart—that apprehends that for which also it is apprehended of God in Christ Jesus.

And now that Satan has been cast out of the heart, and Faith has entered there, what is the next great act in this spiritual drama of the soul? First and next is the outgoing of the soul after Christ, in gratitude and prayer. IMMANUEL is yet *outside*; he must be enshrined within. Hence the description here given, of the whole town, as one man, going forth to thank and praise their great Deliverer, and to invite him within the now empty, and swept, and garnished places of the soul.

We have room for Thee.—All must be filled with a full Christ—Christ with his men and his weapons of war; for even yet there must be the spiritual warfare; not yet has Satan ceased to vex the soul. Diabolonian agents still lurk within; and these are as the uncircumcised of old, dwelling among the people of the Lord, as thorns in their sides, and *to teach them war.* The Canaanite is still in the land. The soul has been recovered and reclaimed, but it must now be *retained* and *held* in the sovereignty of God. Therefore the HOLY WAR must still continue, with its still prolonged history of wars and rumors of wars, and successes and reverses, and loss and gain, until the victory be finally and for ever won.

And in this invitation the soul offers its best and goodliest store to Christ, and dedicates its chiefest and its choicest gifts to his service—"Let it please thee to accept of our *palace* for thy place of residence," etc. The true, believing, loving Christian will present to the Lord, not his meaner gifts, but his greatest gifts; not the lame, and the halt, and the blind, but the firstlings of the flock, and the best of the fold; not the worthless residue of man's wasted influence and exhausted life, but the gold, the frankincense, and the myrrh of truly wise men, whose far travel and patient pilgrimage has had but one only object—to see Jesus, and to worship him.

And when the heart is given to Christ, it is for a yet further discipline. Satan had dwelt within that habitation of the soul, and had wasted and wrecked it by the wear and tear of sin. But Jesus means, by his indwelling, to adorn the house, to beautify the soul, and to glorify the place of his feet. He desires to build it up, to edify it, still more to strengthen it. He enters there *to rule it* by the gentle sway of his all-conquering love; and, by the Holy Spirit's power, to sanctify its thoughts, to purify its motives, to subdue its tempers, to refine its dross, and to conform it in all points to his own mind and will. Satan seeks to mar it, Christ to mend it. DIABOLUS would pull it down; Christ would build it up.

Will you help me?—Among the terms and stipulations of IMMANUEL, one of the foremost is this—"If I come to your town, will you suffer me further to prosecute that which is in my heart against mine enemies and yours? yea, will you *help me* in such undertakings?" Here is Christ pleading with the soul, urging it to count the cost of his indwelling, and making no secret of the terms, the *only* terms, on which he will consent to abide in man. "He must reign." The soul must not only receive of his justifying grace by the full and complete pardon of the past, but it must also undergo the discipline of sanctifying grace, the rough-hewing, it may be, of hard discipline,—any way, the subjugation of the whole man to Christ, the casting down of imaginations, and the abolishing of every idol of the heart.

Come to our Mansoul!—An indwelling Christ is the secret of the Christian's strength, and the only ground of his security. The soul must go out after Christ, and seek for him, and find him. Our bodies are to be the temples of the Holy Ghost; that is, Christ dwelling in our hearts by his Spirit. So long as Christ tarries in the camp outside, the void place of the heart is not filled with the abiding principle of life—"*Christ in you*, the hope of glory."

Hence the earnest and longing anxiety of Mansoul to be possessed of Christ. The townsmen knew what it was to be possessed of Satan; they had felt the spoiler's hand, and had experienced the iron rod of his tyranny. They now desire that *He* should enter there, who had so loved them, and washed them, and adorned them, when they had deserved only death and destruction at his hands. They also rightly put it when they said—"If thou shouldst withdraw, thou and thy captains from us, the town of Mansoul will die." Yes, without Christ the soul must die—"for *He is our life*."

Then he arose and entered Mansoul.—Jesus mounts his car of triumph. The citizens crowd upon the battlements and towers, to witness the in-coming of the King, and to welcome him with shouts of triumph and with songs of gladness. Here are the thoughts and hopes of man, all participating in the universal joy—"Thy King cometh!"

Conducted him into the Castle.—Now the high office and vocation of Captain CREDENCE will appear. This brave Captain had preceded the Prince, with a view to the preparation of the Castle for his Lord's dwelling-place; and, having prepared and made it ready, he must now come forth to conduct the Prince into his resting-place.

This is the description of the exalted office of *Faith*. Christ cannot be received into the heart of man without faith to realize him, and to prepare the man to receive him—"purifying their hearts by faith," Acts 15:9. It is faith that conducts the soul to Christ; it is faith that conducts Christ *to* the soul; it is faith that conducts Jesus *into* the heart.

To receive the whole Army.—Nor does Jesus come alone. His great Captains enter with him, and their ten thousands at their feet. These are "the things that accompany salvation," with all the thousand thoughts, and hopes, and joys, and blessings that follow in their train. And these holy principles are welcomed, and housed, and entertained; and the heart is enlarged to receive them. Accordingly, all the four Captains of SHADDAI and the five Captains of IMMANUEL are duly quartered throughout the soul. INNOCENCE in the reasoning part—the place of intention and forethought. PATIENCE in the mental part—the principle of intelligence. CHARITY in the affectional and emotional part—the place of feeling and sensation. HOPE in the region of the understanding—to enlighten and encourage. BOANERGES and CONVICTION in the conscience—to arouse the soul, and keep it awake. JUDGMENT and EXECUTION in charge over the will—to correct the desires, and to discipline the man. And over all these is Captain CREDENCE—the principle of Faith—abiding in the innermost castle, the Heart. This great motive power of the Christian is never to be lost sight of. Other principles, and gifts, and graces may abide elsewhere, in their own appointed places in the soul; but Faith must occupy the foremost ground, the holiest place of all, the sacred inner shrine. Where Christ is, there Faith must be—"That Christ may dwell in your hearts by faith," Ephesians 3:17.

Immanuel made a Feast.—The feasts and high festivals of the soul are those seasons of special privilege and refreshing which come from the presence of the Lord; including the means of grace, ordinary and extraordinary; the Word of God, broken as the bread of life; the oft-recurring Sabbath-rest for soul and body; the ordinances of the Lord's love; the meditations and contemplations of the reflective mind; the feeding of the hungering and thirsting soul with spiritual food; the daily manna rained round about our habitations; and all other rich supplies of Divine grace and providence.

Oh, what large provision God has made for his world-wide family! He spreads a table for us in the very wilderness, and furnishes the table with the viands of heaven: and "the children must first be fed." This is the privilege of children. Strangers may indirectly benefit by the blessings of Christianity, but God's children are fed and nurtured by the holy feasts of Heaven. Here is reproduced a thousand-fold the miracle of the feeding of the multitudes. The Word of God, given to the soul, and blessed by the benediction of the Son of God, becomes food, spiritual food, enough and to spare, so that the soul is well filled, and it is satisfied.

Some curious riddles.—Under the name of "riddles," Bunyan evidently alludes to *the types* of Holy Scripture. Types are hard riddles, until their answer or meaning is made known; and then they are very easy to be understood—like a complicated lock, impossible to open, until you have got the key. And Christ is the Key of all the types; and in the light of Christ, the anti-type, the guests of Jesus are enabled to say distinctly respecting Christ's nature, and office, and atoning work, "This is the Lamb; this is the Sacrifice; this is the Rock; this is the Red Cow (*i.e.*, the Red Heifer); this is the Door; this is the Way."

And the sequel of this princely entertainment, or, as Bunyan calls it in the margin, "the end of that banquet," deserves attention. It is not every feast that bears reflection as to the end of it; but this heavenly feast, where Jesus entertains his people, is followed by the sweetest thoughts and recollections. Retiring to their homes, the people were all full of holy joy and praise. They did sing of their glorious Prince, and did even talk of him in their sleep. Here are the *thoughts*, and *feelings*, and *recollections* of the renewed soul, ever dwelling upon the manifestation of Jesus in the means of grace, to the great refreshing of the spiritual man. The spiritual food of the Word is to the soul what the provision of food was to the prophet— on the strength of that meat it is enabled to go yet many days.

To new-model the Town.—When we bear in mind the former new-modeling, at the hand of DIABOLUS, we shall all the more appreciate the necessary change now proposed—all things must become new.

Accordingly, IMMANUEL builds strongholds and towers in Mansoul, and fortifies it for himself against rebellion from within, and assault from without. He mounts the "slings" (*i.e.*, the Books of Holy Scrip-ture) in every place. He also invented another instrument of war, for which Bunyan finds no name, but says it was to be worked from the Castle, through Mouth-gate, and to be under the charge of Captain CREDENCE. What might this nameless weapon be? It plainly signifies some spiritual agency, by which the Mouth seconds the suggestion of the Heart, when ruled by Faith. It may mean *Prayer*, which, if it proceed from the heart, as the prayer of faith, is an invincible weapon. Or it may mean, besides, the testimony of the heart of faith, uttered by the lips—"For with the *heart* man believeth unto righteousness; and with *the mouth* confession is made unto salvation," Romans 10:10.

And the officers, also, are new-modeled, so as to bear a holier and better sway over the soul. And first of all is the Will. This part of man's nature is inseparable from man. Whoever may be his master, the Will remains, either to yield submission, or to create and sus-tain resistance. So now, in the renewed man, there is a renewed Will, which receives commission as before, but now for good, over "the walls and gates;"—that is, over the "flesh" and the "senses." The Understanding, too, is restored to office, as Lord Mayor, with a palace adjoining Eye-gate. This is a contrast to former times, when the Understanding was darkened; for now he is appointed to dwell in the light, and in the place of clear perception. And this is neces-sary, in as much as his future office involves the careful study of the *mysteries* of God, so that he may be able to interpret or explain them to the soul.

And KNOWLEDGE becomes Recorder—another and higher office

being reserved for CONSCIENCE. Knowledge is now to be the soul's remembrancer—"This is life eternal, that they might *know* thee the only true God, and Jesus Christ, whom thou hast sent," John 17:3. He that walks in the light of this knowledge need never go astray.

The soul is now represented as dealing thoroughly with the evil and corrupt nature. Bonds and imprisonment await the lusts, and passions, and corruptions of the "old man." Truth, under the name of TRUE-MAN, holds watch and ward over these elements of the carnal mind, bringing the soul into subjection to the law of Christ. The strongholds of DIABOLUS are now dismantled of their terrors, and utterly razed to the ground. The Hold-of-Defiance no longer commands the town with its sweeping range. Midnight-Hold is leveled in the dust, no longer darkening the prospect, but opening up a broad way for the free light of heaven. And Sweet-Sin-Hold gives way to a better defense of the soul—the "desire of good."

CHAPTER VII

SERVING ONE MASTER

OUTLINE OF CHAPTER VII.—Trial and Condemnation of the Diabo-
lonians.—The Judge, Jury, and Witnesses.—The Prisoners: Mr.
Atheism, Mr. Lustings, Mr. Incredulity, Mr. Forget-Good, Mr. Hard-
Heart, Mr. False-Peace, Mr. No-Truth, Mr. Pitiless, Mr. Haughty.—
The Charge.—The Verdict.—The Execution.—Escape of Mr. Incre-
dulity, who still survives.—His Report to Diabolus, his Master.

Trial and Execution of the Diabolonians.—Mansoul is now serving one
Master; this is the decision of the soul. Accordingly, after the old
officers have been restored, the image of DIABOLUS destroyed, and the
image of SHADDAI set up, the discipline of the soul begins, the searching of the reins of the heart, and the casting out of the residue of
Satan's power. The difference must never be lost sight of between
the Diabolonians and the native-born. The one class is to be renewed, reformed, restored; the other is to be exterminated, cast out,
and utterly destroyed. The continuance of the HOLY WAR is, in fact,
the life of the Christian man, striving and struggling against either
and both of these elements. And so, consistently with the new
service of the soul, the lurking Diabolonian powers are now brought
forth for examination, condemnation, and execution.

The three principal witnesses seem to be suggestive of the mod-
ern form of oath in courts of law—KNOW-ALL indicating the facts of
the case—"the truth;" TELL-TRUE including all the facts—"the whole
truth;" and HATE-LIES binding the witness to state nothing that is
false—"nothing but the truth."

The subsequent narrative, interwoven into the Allegory, sufficiently explains itself. The names of all the parties concerned are so
significant and suggestive as to render the story its own best interpreter. The Diabolonians under judgment, the jury that is empanelled, the witnesses that bear evidence, are all so many principles
personified; principles of the renewed heart sitting in judgment on
the Old Man. The whole scene is laid before us as a practical illustration of the earnest effort of the faithful soul to rid itself of the

living power of Satan, by careful search after evil principles, and the utter extinction of the evil nature, when found lurking in the spiritual man. "Search me, O God, and know my heart; try me, and know my thoughts; and see if there be any wicked way in me, and lead me in the way everlasting," Psalm 139:23–24.

ATHEISM is first arraigned—the principle of Unbelief that dwells in man by reason of his carnal nature. It does not mean the spirit of Atheism embodied in a form, or wrought into a system of Infidelity, but rather that practical unconcern evinced by so many in the matter of religion, and of relationship to God.

In these examinations, the soul is its own witness. Memory and conscience look back upon the past, and bring out of their treasure-house the accusations of the soul against the evil principles that once suggested thoughts of sin, motives of unbelief, and whisperings of infidelity. The renewed man remembers all these, and fearing lest they should again resume their sway, he desires utterly to destroy the spirit of evil. And, first of all must be established the existence and sovereignty of that God, who has propounded a holy law, which is to regulate man's thoughts and deeds. Man would escape from this great truth if he could; but no, the spirit of Atheism must be destroyed.

LUSTINGS is the body of the flesh—the carnal instrument of so much loss and damage to the soul; it is the law in our members warring against the law of the mind. This evil spirit remains long after Satan has been cast out. It is the inner nature, still untamed. It must be searched out, examined, convicted, mortified, crucified, utterly slain—"the body of this death." It is to the renewed man what the dead body would be when, as in olden times, bound to a living man—"Oh, wretched man, that I am! who shall deliver me from the body of this death?" Romans 7:24.

The unrenewed man, in whom this evil element bears sway, knows no restraint; sin *reigns* in his mortal body; and through its influence the spirit is carnalised, and brought into weary bondage. It needs the true and unflinching witness of the heart to expose the workings of this indwelling foe, to crucify this Old Man with its affections and lusts.

Bunyan's descriptions of the prisoners respectively are true to nature. Here, for example, is LUSTINGS associated with those features and circumstances by which Lust is generally and best known in human experience. Although this evil passion of the soul is confined to no particular class of men, yet it rules with greatest power where there is fullness of bread, and abundance of pleasure, and supera-bundance of the good things of this life. These things lead to indul-gence, luxury, and excess; and when the carnal nature is thus fed with fullness, and thus lies in the lap of luxury, and its cup of wrath runneth over, it departs from God more and more, and is given to "filthiness and the superfluity of naughtiness."

Lust also leads to further evils; and it seems but a light thing to speak words of blasphemy and falsehood, and to forget God, and his Holy Word, and his Holy Day. It is, in fact, the *abandon* of the soul to "the wretchlessness of unclean living," which is, indeed, a most dangerous downfall. And this evil principle glories in its shame; it is its nature, and its desire, and its great pleasure thus to defile the man. It casts a loose rein upon the flowing mane of the roaring lion, which hurries the soul a-down the steep incline, that leads to hell.

INCREDULITY—once the spirit of defense and of defiance of the soul—openly avows his hatred of the King, and his still unaltered and unalterable determination to serve DIABOLUS, his master. So long as this principle remains, it continues to be a spiritual hindrance to the soul. Unbelief does not yield obedience to Christ, and will not change or reform its nature. It is well, therefore, it should be destroyed.

Incredulity is the spirit of direct antagonism against the law of God; and to the last it chooses to serve Satan, and to abide under the standard of the Evil One. Incredulity seeks to gain dominion over the *minds* of men, sometimes inducing them to imagine that it is a *manly* thing to doubt and disbelieve. This spirit in man is a chief agent of Satan; and how essential it is to the continuance of his dominion here, will appear by and by. Meanwhile, Incredulity lacks not words of bold and brazen confidence, to justify its measure of evil influence over the human mind.

FORGET-GOOD—the Diabolonian Recorder—is the besetting sin of most men. It thinks and reflects on evil, and forgets the good—

> "The evil things it writes on stone,
> The good it writes on water!"

It catches at the straws that float upon the surface, and gives no heed to the weightier matters, and more abiding good, hidden beneath the waters of the stream. This spirit of forgetfulness lays up no store of good and holy thoughts, no treasures of a consecrated memory, no remembrance of the Holy Word. The soul is utterly empty and void of all supply for Christian meditation, contempla-tion, and waiting upon God.

The soul that is "forgetful" of God would excuse itself by reason of its "infirmity" and "weakness," as though its offence were more of a passive than of an active character. No doubt it means the spiritual indolence of the soul, giving itself no care, diligence, or exercise in the things of God, and thus allowing many things to fall through, and escape from memory; yet this very spirit of indolence is an active agent of the soul's decline. Men ofttimes try to forget, and put themselves to much ingenuity and industry, in order to banish the thoughts of God and of good from the mind and memory. It involves, as indeed Bunyan's argument would suggest, the successive stages of an active process—the doing violence to the Conscience, the casting it out of office, and debauching of its character, ere the soul can entertain the principle of spiritual "forgetfulness." The evidence of TELL-TRUE argues an active effort on the part of the soul to get rid of holy thoughts—"I have heard him often say he would rather think of the vilest thing, than of what is contained in the Holy Scriptures."

HARD-HEART is, of a truth, a Diabolonian principle. It knows not what remorse or sorrow is; it feels nothing; no impulse pierces through this hard iron breast-plate. Others may weep, but Hard-Heart never weeps; others may feel, but Hard-Heart can not sympathize with any. Of such a one it may be said—"His heart is as firm as a stone; yea, as hard as a piece of the nether millstone," Job 41:24.

A sympathizing heart is one of the marks of the better nature—it is essentially Christ-like. The all-compassionate Savior has left this example to his followers, that they should imitate and copy him. But the more we possess of Satan's spirit, the harder does the heart become—a stony heart, unimpressible by outer objects, impervious to the holy influences of either Divine or human love, all-unconscious of the blessedness which is the portion of the compassionate and loving heart—

> "The heart that's moved with love to God
> With love to man will glow."

FALSE-PEACE is the voice that whispers peace, peace, where there is no peace! This is the false principle that lulls so many souls to rest, and sings their lullaby while tempests roar. It whispered false-peace to Sodom; it rocked the guilty prophet to sleep, while fleeing from the command of God; and in the very midst of the war with Mansoul, False-peace was ever busied about his master's Diabolonian business. "What peace, so long as the whoredoms of thy mother Jezebel and her witchcrafts are so many?" 2 Kings 9:22.

False-Peace is the self-deception of the soul, the traitor within the camp—"A deceived heart hath turned him aside." Sin is set forth under the garb of righteousness, and vice under the name of virtue. It needs, indeed, the examination and cross-examination of the heart to draw forth this element from its disguise, and to declare its true nature before all men. It needs both the indefatigable diligence of SEARCH-TRUTH, and the unerring witness of VOUCH-TRUTH, to know and to discover the treacherous character of FALSE-PEACE. It is, verily, Satan clothing himself as an angel of light, deceiving, if it were possible, the very elect of God.

The ingenuity of this principle is evidenced by the crafty attempt to ignore his own proper name, and to call himself by the name of PEACE. The heart, which is "deceitful above all things, and desperately wicked," would flatter itself in its own eyes, and indulge the imagination of the heart that all is well. There are two passages of Scripture which would suffice to show from whence springs this self-deceiving spirit: St. Paul traces it to an over-weening *estimation of self*—"If a man think himself to be something, when he is nothing, he deceiveth himself," Galatians 6:3. And St. James implies that it arises from *forgetfulness of self*—"If any be a hearer of the word, and not a doer, he is like unto a man beholding his natural face in a glass: for he beholdeth himself, and goeth his way, and straightway forgetteth what manner of man he was," James 1:23–24.

The principle of False-peace, then, blinds the eyes and perverts the judgment of man, and also causes him to forget what manner of man he really is. He looks, he sees, he departs, and he forgets. This is self-deception. God has supplied to us a mirror of personal inspection and observation—his Holy Word. In this mirror we may see ourselves reflected. Our character is truthfully represented there, either in example or description. If the Word should speak peace, it is peace indeed; but if we forget our true state as revealed to us in that truthful mirror, then are we the victims of False-peace.

The remedy against this spirit of self-deception and false-peace is this:—Take the mirror of the Word as you would take any other mirror. Take it thankfully as an opportunity for beholding yourself. Take it as your companion to your closet, where none but God can see, where none but God is near. In the secrecy of closet meditation, avail yourself of this opportunity of amendment, such as does not exist outside, or elsewhere. Neglect this, and all shall be discovered in open day; and what thou hast whispered in thine ear in secret, if despised, will ere long be proclaimed upon the house-top. "The day shall declare it."

When FALSE-PEACE is permitted to call himself PEACE in your ears, you are deceiving your own selves, and being deceived. Then, make inquiry, bring the self-deceiving principle to judgment within your own heart, and utterly uproot him from the occupancy of the soul. Use the timely instruction and admonition of the spiritual mirror. Let not self-deception any longer deceive. In that all-important hour remove the blemish and the blame, that they be not seen outside. Many mistakes may be corrected by private drill and discipline, when honestly conducted, in the light of honest day. Only, let not False-peace blind your eyes, darken your understanding, pervert your judgment, and thus bring you into condemnation.

NO-TRUTH is that principle of the reprobate mind that strives to banish God from even the thought of the heart. It was this element of the soul that destroyed the image and erased the superscription of SHADDAI from the gates, and set up the image of DIABOLUS. When this rabid form of sin lays hold upon the heart, it seeks to destroy every trace and vestige of even the remembrance of God. Well is it for the soul when it gains the mastery over this element of the carnal nature.

Deep indeed must have been the downfall and degradation of Mansoul when such a principle as this obtained authority and power—thus to do violence to the King of all, thus to deface his image, thus to obliterate his superscription, thus to erase all traces of the thought of God from the soul. It is part of the decisive action of Satan, part of the determined mastery with which he rules in man. It is an evidence of the ruin of the soul, its far distant departure from the righteousness of God, and the apparent helplessness and hopelessness of its condition—thus "bound and sold under sin." When the soul is thus wholly possessed of the power of the great DIABOLUS, it is plunged into that lowest level of condemnation of which Jesus speaks in the hearing of the unbelieving Jews:—"Ye are of your father the devil, and the lusts of your father ye will do. He was a murderer from the beginning, and abode not in the truth, because there is *no truth* in him," John 8:44.

PITILESS is that character of the carnal mind that is devoid of feeling and compassion for the soul in its degraded and desolate condition. It would make the best of its worst estate, and, rather than the soul should sink into sorrow and melancholy for its sin, would administer false joy, false hope, and false peace. Sorrow might lead the soul to repentance, and therefore the spirit of Diabolus enters in to soothe and cheer it, though in the midst of danger and death.

The character and nature of this principle, according to Bunyan's intention, would appear from the plea of the accused—"My name is not Pitiless, but Cheer-Up; and I could not abide to see Mansoul incline to melancholy." This is another of those elements of spiritual bravado that sometimes settle down upon the spirit of man, restraining repentance, quenching conviction, and resisting the strivings of the Spirit of God. Under such influence the soul is hardened, the conscience seared, and the whole man deceived. Satan sends his messenger to effect the diversion of the mind, the dissipation of conscience; hushing the awakened sinner back to his deep sleep again, or rallying the troubled heart from its terror and its fear, that it be not utterly consumed of sorrow.

The spirit of the world, and the feelings of the flesh, ofttimes discharge this duty for Satan. How often has sorrow, which seemed to be "godly sorrow," failed of its purpose, and wrought no repentance, because of the intervention of the worldly mind and the spirit of worldliness. How many a bud of promise has been crushed in its birth, or prematurely blighted by the intrusion of pleasure, appetite and lust? How many souls have been lost by reason of the "pitiless" spirit that transforms our holy sorrow into un-holy cheer, stupefying or intoxicating the soul with the wine-cup of indifference and unconcern!

Haughty is the name by which the spirit of carnal pride is indicated—the "heady, high-minded" spirit of the soul, that will not bend its neck to the yoke of Christ, or yield itself to the obedience of Christ. This is the alleged "manliness" of unbelief, the vaunted "spirit" of scepticism, that makes a scoff at all religion, and speaks contemptuously of those who walk in religion's ways. To brave the threatenings of God, and brazen out the protests of his law; to mouth the heavens, and charge God foolishly; to vaunt a boasted valiancy, and flaunt a defiant flag—these seem to be the sum and substance of this "brave man's" doings. He has never descended to the well-watered level of the valley of humility, where goodly fruits and flowers are found, but has climbed the sides of the barren rock, and sought the eminence of the mountain height, the region of perpetual frost and of everlasting snow. He has ventured high; his fall shall be deep:—"Pride goeth before destruction, and an haughty spirit before a fall," Proverbs 16:18.

The Charge.—After the several indictments had been delivered, the pleas of the prisoners spoken, and the witnesses examined, the whole question is referred to the empanelled jury, who are directed to withdraw for the consideration of their verdict.

Here is the soul represented as withdrawing into itself—into the secret chamber of the heart and conscience, sitting in judgment upon the Diabolonian passions, and feelings, and appetites of the man. Through a process of self-examination it has brought to light the principles of the evil nature, the elements of antagonism to Divine things, those deadly instruments of Satan that war against the soul. All the evidence is now to be reviewed, and the issue determined.

If we would know ourselves, we must examine ourselves. There is no thorough attainment of self-knowledge without a thorough self-examination. Existent evil and indwelling sin must be searched for, and sought out, and brought to trial and condemnation. For an honest process of self-inquiry there must needs be proving, probing, seeking and searching with diligence, face to face with one's own self, directing the eye of the understanding full upon the inner man. This being done, it remains for the holy principles of the renewed soul to bring in their verdict; and for the enlightened Understanding, the certified Knowledge, the instructed Conscience, and the renewed Will, to receive that verdict, and act accordingly.

THE VERDICT.—The conclave of holy principles, now in close communion in the soul, express their several opinions, and then conjoin them all in one sentence—of Death. Mr. BELIEF presides over this counsel of the soul; and thus *faith* is again honored as a chief power in the renewed man. Each principle expresses its sentence in the direction of its own nature, showing how many reasons the soul has for the treading down of the flesh, and the slaying of the corrupt and carnal nature; and the verdict is the unanimous sentence of the principles of the heart—all are agreed as to the necessity of "putting off the body of the sins of the flesh."

A striking contrast is suggested by this scene in the HOLY WAR, namely, the trial and condemnation of CHRISTIAN and FAITHFUL, in Vanity Fair, as related in the PILGRIM'S PROGRESS. There the names of all the parties concerned were likewise significant of so many principles. It was the world, and the spirit of the world, and sin, and pleasure sitting in judgment upon the renewed nature and causing men to suffer persecution and the loss of all things, for the sake of Christ. The pen of Bunyan has proved equally felicitous in the description of this scene, though the actual examination is more prolonged; so much so, that unless we appreciate its deep spiritual meaning, we might charge it with unnecessary sameness and needless repetition. If, however, we view it in its true light, we will

see that it is one of the most important portions of the book, pointing out the manifold lurking foes of the spiritual man, and how
necessary it is to examine and cross-examine, and diligently to
guard against being self-deceived in the process.

The atheistic spirit, the spirit of lust, the unbelieving incredulity
of man, the heart forgetful of all good, the hard-heart, the spirit of
false-peace, the enmity of no-truth, the pitiless character of the
sinner, and the haughty pride of the carnal nature—these, and such
as these, are the convicted enemies of God and man—the evil
principles of the carnal mind. They must all be arraigned, and
brought to judgment, and tried. Weighed in the righteous balance,
they are all found wanting; and, accordingly, the righteous sentence
must go forth—"Guilty of death!"

And this sentence must be followed up by prompt and speedy
execution; else the Diabolonian principles survive, and this would
be for further loss and damage to the soul. Trial and condemnation
are of no avail unless enforced by final execution. It is not enough to
punish the carnal nature; not enough to correct it; not enough to
prune its excesses, or to cut it down—it must be plucked up, rooted
out, utterly destroyed, root and branch. The smallest seed of evil left
in the soil of the human heart is the germ of future sin, and may be
the secret cause of eternal death.

Another bold and masterly stroke of Bunyan's pen is that in
which he describes the escape of INCREDULITY; and, indeed, he still
survives, in many forms and fashions, as well in the church as in
the world; and he survives for mischief. He is the *confidante* of
DIABOLUS, and informs his master of the doings of the soul. It is the
principle of unbelief in man that holds intercourse with Satan; it is
from man's unbelief that Satan learns all about the soul—how it
fares; whether it be strong or weak; and whether it is inclined the
more to Satan or to God.

All the full tale of loss is now told to DIABOLUS by the escaped prisoner, INCREDULITY. If there is any emanation of the renewed soul
going out after Satan, it is the spirit of Unbelief. Otherwise, Satan
would be utterly cut off from any further connection with the soul of
the renewed man. If ever the bond of union is bound again, it is
man's unbelief that binds it. It is the remnant of sin, the escaped
fugitive of the carnal nature, a principle that is permitted still to
live, for the further probation of the Christian man. Well may the
best of us say, "Lord, I believe; help thou mine *unbelief!*"

THE EXECUTION.—This is the great issue—the only safe issue of the strife and struggle of the soul against its spiritual foes. For this was the renovated soul re-possessed by the power of Christ; for this was the vigilance of the soul awakened; for this were the detectives of the inner man sent forth to search out the lurking sins in their secret hiding-places; for this were the principles of the carnal nature brought to the judgment-seat; for this were they tried; and for this were they condemned. The Christian man would be false to his own conviction, would belie the evidence of proof, would contravene the testimony of many witnesses, would be inconsistent with his own judgment, would stultify his own decision, would be blind to his own interest, and would forfeit the favor of his God and King, if, after such a process of self-examination and self-condemnation, he were to hesitate to fulfill the sentence to the letter, and utterly to abolish the whole body of sin.

The execution of the Diabolonian principles is intended to represent the dying and the slaying of sin within us. Our spiritual life and well-being depend upon this utter extermination of the spiritual foe; for if we do not slay him, he will slay us. "For if ye live after the flesh, ye shall die: but if ye through the Spirit do mortify the deeds of the body, ye shall live," Romans 8:13. This is both the duty and the interest of the renewed man—"They that are Christ's have crucified the flesh with the affections and lusts," Galatians 5:24.

Accordingly, to the Cross the evil principles are conducted; and yet it is hard work to slay them. Sins are "die-hards." They make strong resistance, even to the last. And, at length, it is only by the assistance of Divine grace, and by the power of the Holy Spirit, that the complete discomfiture is accomplished. And God, by his Spirit, will help the soul to slay its spiritual foes; and in this great fight He will "strengthen such as do stand, and comfort and help the weak-hearted, and raise up them that fall, and finally beat down Satan under our feet."

CHAPTER VIII

THE NEW CHARTER

OUTLINE OF CHAPTER VIII.—Promotions and Appointments.—Rights and Privileges Established.—The Ministry of Mansoul.—The Lord Chief Secretary (the Holy Spirit), the Chief Teacher.—Conscience appointed as Preacher and Adviser to Mansoul.—Gifts and Cautions: Hold fast by Shaddai's Captains; Beware of lurking Diabolonians; Give heed to the appointed Ministry of Mansoul.—Gift of White Robes.—Instructed how to keep them.—Immanuel's Standard set up.—Daily Visits of the Prince.—His High Festivals.—The New Governor of Mansoul.—Mr. God's-Peace.

The Prince came down to see.—The faithful service of the soul is not forgotten before God. The one heart, given unreservedly to Christ, is the prelude to great and precious privileges, arising from the mutual indwelling—Christ in us, and we in Christ; "Ye in me, and I in you." Many favors are associated with the residence of a king; his house is a palace, and, wherever he may tarry, there he makes presents of goodly and costly things, and leaves mementoes of his visit. And surely the abiding of Christ in the soul must involve the presentation of tokens of his favor, and the possession of many things not otherwise to be attained.

The jealousy of the "jealous God" is satisfied of the soul's true love by reason of the execution of the Diabolonian leaders. The casting out of these—lust, and unbelief, and hardness of heart, and false peace—leaves Christ the acknowledged Ruler of the heart, the indwelling Lord of Mansoul.

Make them another captain.—As in ordinary usage, after a conflict and victory, promotions are made, and new officers created; so now, in the warfare of the soul, rewards and distinctions are bestowed upon those principles that have been most valiant in the fight. The first of these rewards is granted to Mr. EXPERIENCE, who had served under Captain CREDENCE. Here is the experience of the soul enlarged and made more honorable. This principle is educated and brought up under the tuition of Faith, in the school of test and trial—

"Tribulation worketh patience, and patience experience;" and having endured hardness, and proved itself a good soldier, it is now promoted to the chief rank in the soul.

The Experience of the man of God, the good soldier of the cross, counts for something in the estimation of God. To the soul experience is indispensable; it is the knowledge, and, as such, the guide of the soul—the knowledge of God, in Christ, through the Spirit; the knowledge of God's dealings with the soul, and of the soul's dealings with itself, and of Satan's manifold temptations; the ups and downs, the reverses and successes, of the long continued strife, and all the diversified phases of the battle of the warrior. And as Faith marches on, and fights the good fight, Experience is enlarging, increasing, ripening, maturing, and thus becoming more and more useful to the Christian soldier; and in proportion to its use and increase, it is honorable and honored in God's sight, and receives fresh tokens of his favor and approval.

Christian Experience is well represented here as having been once subordinate to Faith. The connection of these two principles may be thus stated—faith is the root, experience is the bringing forth of the fruit; faith is the foundation, experience is the superstructure; faith is the seed, experience is the development of the seed; faith is the food of the soul, experience is the digestion of the food, turning it into bone, and muscle, and sinew of the man of God, thoroughly furnished unto all good works.

Soundeth his trumpet for volunteers.—Well and worthily was this principle promoted to a chief command, and soon did EXPERIENCE gather a goodly company. The thoughts, and hopes, and feelings of the good man rejoice to rally round the standard of experience. The names of the subalterns of this Captain are suggestive of a goodly group of Christian talents, indicating the value of Christian knowledge and skill, and the work of the renewed memory as the treasure-house of the renewed heart. Experience is made up of *knowledge*, of things found out and learned; *memory*, storing them up for after use in time of need; and *skill*, in the choice of the best and most useful lessons, with power to make the best use of them in every season of test and trial. Life is the great school of experience, God's word the text-book of the school, and the Holy Spirit the teacher of all that resort thither. To know God more and more, to serve him better and better, to advance to further stages of knowledge—these are the great purposes to be gained by Christian experience, the earnest aim and steadfast desire of every renewed heart; and short of these attainments, no true Christian can possibly be satisfied.

The dead lion and the dead bear.—This was the escutcheon of Experience, in allusion to the brave exploits of David, the remembrance of which gave him courage to meet the Philistine. God had delivered him from the lion and the bear; he remembered this deliverance, and thus his experience told him that God could still deliver him. Experience is the far-travelled principle of the soul, that has trod the road, and measured the way, and realized the dangers and difficulties of the path, and learned how to meet them and to surmount them. A retentive memory and a skilful hand are the executive of Experience.

Renew their charter.—New rights, new immunities, new claims are now granted to Mansoul, which, with an indwelling Christ, becomes the chartered city of the great King. The new charter secures to the soul many high and glorious privileges, which the renewed man shall have and enjoy, so long as Immanuel inhabits the heart.

This holy charter is the deed of spiritual enfranchisement, by which the soul is not only set free from its former bondage, but is also invested with peculiar rights and privileges, including—

1. The amnesty of the past—forgiveness, free, full, and for ever. All that was wrong under Satan's sovereignty is set right under the governance of Christ.

2. The gift of the Word for comfort and consolation—"the comfort of the Scriptures." The possession of chartered rights involves the discharge of rightful duties. Hence the gift of the Law and holy Testament for direction, counsel, admonition, and consolation.

3. The gift of grace—as to Christ, in its fullness; so to us, of the same grace, but by measure,—"And of his fullness have all we received, and grace for grace."

4. Power over the world—to tread it beneath their feet. Man was originally created with a design that he should be the lord over things temporal. Accordingly, the commission given to him was—"Be fruitful, and multiply, and replenish the earth, and *subdue it,*" Genesis 1:28. By man's rebellion, this dominion was lost; but in Christ it is once more restored to man's possession.

5. Free and ready access to the King at his royal house in all dangers and adversities, the privilege of audience, and the promise of redress. God's servants are also his children, with the privilege of filial boldness, in their approach to a loving Father, who has promised them a true welcome to his house.

6. Dominion over the flesh and all carnal things, and liberty to

destroy the lurking power of Satan in the soul. This is the duty as well as the interest of the renewed heart. The measure of the enjoyment of this holy charter will be in proportion as the evil and corrupt nature is restrained, kept down, and destroyed within us.

7. The reservation of the rights of citizenship and freedom to the natives only, to the utter exclusion for ever of the Diabolonians. The new charter was not for the "old man," but for the "new man which is created anew in Christ Jesus."

This charter is proclaimed to the soul by the Recorder (KNOWLEDGE), and is then engraved upon the Castle (the Heart). God's covenant of peace with man is brought home to the heart, through Knowledge, and is then imprinted on the heart as with a pen of iron. Through the *head* God reaches the *heart* of his people.

Establish a ministry among them.—This involves an essential step in the interest of the soul. The Christian man, in the school of Christ, is a disciple, desiring to learn more and more, and to be more fully instructed in these matters. He therefore needs instructors and teachers; and, accordingly, two prime teachers are provided. One of these is from heaven, and the other is on earth. The human and the Divine were blended together in Christ, and now the Divine and human are combined in the teaching of Christ's people.

The Divine Teacher is the Holy Spirit. Being co-equal with the Father, the Spirit knows the mysteries of God's mind, and is the only Teacher of supernatural truth. The great work of the chief Minister is, to take of the things of God, and to show them unto us; to teach, and instruct, and lead us into all truth; to suggest what petitions we should offer; to put life into the dead, to give sight unto the blind, and to sanctify and bless the people of God. It is for man to take heed that nothing shall enter the soul without the express permission of this high ruling power, lest he should thereby grieve the Holy Spirit of God, the chief Teacher of Mansoul.

Conscience is the human minister—the once Recorder of the soul. The conscience of the renewed man is not a prime teacher, but a subordinate minister. It is the monitor of the soul in all moral, civil, and natural duties. This teacher's office is limited and dependent, owing all its power and vigor to the chief Teacher—the Holy Spirit.

This ready-reckoner of the soul is an indwelling, ever-present monitor to man, and wields an irresistible power. What was it that drove Adam and his wife from the converse of their God, to seek a hiding-place amid the bowers of Eden? It was Conscience! Why did Cain feel his punishment to be greater than he could bear? and why was he thus sad, and his countenance fallen? It was because of Conscience! Why did the infatuated Pharaoh again and again relent of his cruel policy regarding Israel? It was by reason of Conscience! What influence was it that impelled the now-forsaken Saul to inquire of the witch of Endor, and to ask that she would fetch up Samuel to him from the grave? It was the working of a restless Conscience, because "the Lord answered him not, neither by dreams, nor by Urim, nor by prophets." Whence cometh it that men, as David says, "were in great fear, where no fear was?" and as Solomon says—"the wicked flee when no man pursueth?"—is it not from the power of Conscience? What was the cause of that sudden panic that seized hold upon Belshazzar, when, amid his nobles, and in the banqueting-hall of his festivity, "the king's countenance was changed, and his thoughts troubled him?" It was the power of Conscience, that distinctly traced and read the mysterious writing on the wall, and saw therein the sentence of his condemnation. Why did Judas cast the price of his treason at the feet of the chief priests, and then go and hang himself? Oh, how sorely smitten! his Conscience constrained him thus to act. And why did Felix tremble before the preaching of Paul, but because of the terrors of Conscience, which awakened in all their power, while the Apostle "reasoned of righteousness, temperance, and judgment to come?" All Scripture is eloquent, from first to last, with vivid descriptions of the admonitory power of Conscience.

Conscience is not only a monitor, but also a teacher, a leader, and a guide to man; and, when it is under the influence of the sanctifying Spirit, it is a safe guide. The power of Conscience ought to be exercised *before* the doing of the deed. If men would only allow an enlightened Conscience to anticipate their acts, they would suffer less from its subsequent chastisements. Let Conscience dictate; then is the deed its own, and it will not condemn the doer of it. Conscience, instructed from above, has its law within itself, "written in the heart." Here, then, is a teacher and a judge, continually instructed by an ever-present law, having its rule of direction not afar off, but nigh at hand—in the very heart of man. This teacher must be jealously guarded as to the source of its instruction, lest it should unduly and unfaithfully execute the functions of its office.

A necessary caution.—The soul possessed by an indwelling Christ, chartered and enfranchised in its new liberty and recovered rights, instructed by a twofold ministry (human and Divine), is now yet more enlarged; gifts and graces are more abundantly bestowed, and yet more augmented. These new gifts involve new responsibilities, and therefore consequent cautions are given to the soul that it should *keep* its gifts securely, and *use* them well and wisely. To such newly-chartered souls it may be said, "All things are yours; and ye are Christ's," 1 Corinthians 3:21–23.

1. The first caution is respecting the five captains: they have been admitted and received; they must now be welcomed, entertained, respected, and never permitted to depart. These five captains represent the graces of the Spirit in the renewed soul. They come with Christ; they enter with Christ; they tarry where Christ abides. Faith, Hope, Charity, Patience, Innocence—how holy the heart in which they are found; and how important to keep them there! These principles are more tender and more sensitive than the first four captains. BOANERGES and his comrades are rough-hewn men, that fight their way, and are able to bear the brunt of opposition and resistance; their duty is to resist, and oppose, and earnestly to contend. But not so these more delicate principles—the graces of the soul; they must be welcomed, and be ever made to *feel* that they are welcome; and only according as the true welcome is given and favor showed, do they abide with men.

These graces, we have already seen, have been quartered on the various principles of the soul—the reason, mind, affection, heart, and understanding. It now devolves upon these principles to entertain their heavenly guests; and according to the measure of their entertainment, are they strong or weak. Sometimes the indwelling grace is feeble and sickly: the pulse of Faith low; Hope and Love faint; Patience weary; and Innocence offended or defiled. Therefore they must be all the more delicately tended. If they are weak, they must be made strong; if sickly, they must be made well; for they are everything to Mansoul. Their weakness is the soul's weakness; their strength is the soul's strength.

In this timely caution, Bunyan means to illustrate the warfare of the body against the soul; the holy and heavenly principles in man beset with daily danger, enduring a great fight of affliction, and scarcely holding their own in the face of opposition from without and from within. The graces of the Spirit are exotics here, planted in an ungenial soil, surrounded by an unfriendly atmosphere. They must therefore be gently tended and cared for; otherwise they can but pine and waste away, as lone strangers in a desert land.

2. The second caution has reference to the Diabolonians still lurking in the soul. Even with IMMANUEL in the heart, the power of

DIABOLUS is not wholly exterminated from the soul. Sins do not, indeed, dwell within the *heart*, if Christ be there; but they linger about the walls, and lurk in holes, and dens, and caves. Banished from the heart, sin still abides in the body, the members, the flesh, and the circumstances of man. Hence this timely caution—IMMANUEL advertises the soul of the continued survival of these principles; tells their names and their lurking-places; bids the soul to look in the law of the God, as in a looking-glass, and there to see itself and its spiritual state, and to know the things that antagonize the soul, and bring it low into subjection and captivity.

Hence the full powers invested in the Christian man—to execute summary judgment on all such, to slay them, to continue still to crucify the old man, to mortify the whole body of sin, and to spare nothing that appertains to the spiritual Amalek, but "to go and smite them, and utterly destroy all that they have," (1 Samuel 15:3).

A further badge of honor.—The investiture of the renewed soul is not yet completed. God will yet more abundantly make known his own children. Hence the description of new badges and distinctions, whereby the soul is set apart for Christ, so that the world may know, and that the *soul itself* may know, that it is the Lord's.

The "white robes" are the righteousness of Christ—the fair linen with which God clothes his people—robes not purchased by us, but freely given by him. And clad in this fair, white dress, the soul is all-glorious—"fair as the sun"—in that imputed righteousness, which shines in its own perfect glory, all light and no darkness at all; "clear as the moon"—in that imparted righteousness, the sancti-fication of the Spirit, ever crescent, increasing, and going on to perfection; and "terrible as an army with banners" in the conflicts and conquests, the trials and the triumphs, of the justified and sanctified believer.

And the special gift of these fair robes involves special cautions:—

1. *Wear them daily;* not on Sundays only, but on all days. There is no mere Sunday garb for Christians; they must always be in court dress. There is no furlough for the Christian soldier; he must always be in armor. The daily dress of the Christian is as essential as the Christian's "daily bread."

2. *Keep them white;* even though you must walk through unclean places, yet keep the garments clean and unspotted from the world. They are presented white as snow; and white as snow must they be after life's long journey, after the mire and clay of this naughty world, and after the dust and defilement of the hard-fought battle-field.

3. *Gird them up;* the long-flowing robes of the ancients were gathered up from the dust and the mire, and girt about the loins, so as
not to entangle the feet. The Christian pilgrim may thus walk
better and cleaner. Hence the allusion of St. Paul—"Let us lay aside
every weight, and the sin which doth so easily beset us, and let us
run with patience the race that is set before us," Hebrews 12:1. And
again, another apostle—"Wherefore gird up the loins of your mind,"
1 Peter 1:13.

4. *Lose them not;* lest you be found naked, and the shame of sin
and your spiritual poverty be made known. Rags are for the City of
Destruction, not for the onward journey of the Pilgrim.

5. *If you soil them, wash them clean again;* there is a cleansing fountain ever open. Fear to sin, or to soil the robe; but if it be soiled, fear
not nor be ashamed to acknowledge the sin, and again to seek the
washing of the Spirit.

These gifts and cautions given, then is the soul filled with gladness—redeemed, restored, enfranchised, honored, clothed, and
made strong by IMMANUEL for himself; or, as Bunyan sums up the full
tale of this high privilege and glory, "Mansoul has now a most
excellent Prince, golden captains and men of war, weapons proved,
and garments as white as snow!"

And then, etc.—The sequel of this glorious investiture is, that
Jesus draws nearer and nearer to the soul in close communion and
intercourse. His visits are seasons of refreshing. Is the soul weak?
his touch makes it strong. Is it sickly? his healing word restores it.
Is it hungry? he feeds it with heavenly food. So that, by-and-by,
every day becomes a feast-day to the soul, with its provisions
specially sent from the royal table.

The soul is thus described as being filled with all joy and peace in
believing. Her God is in the midst of her, and the shout of a King is
in her camp. Her chief delight now is in communion with the Prince,
who meets his beloved "in all the streets, gardens, orchards"—the
fruitful places of the soul's refreshment, and thus pervades *the whole
man*, visiting, and by his visits sanctifying all the thoughts, and
feelings, and principles of the soul. "Out of *the heart* are the issues of
life;" and this is true spiritually as well as physically. As Christ
dwells in the heart, and sends forth the pulses of spiritual life from
the heart, so do the thoughts, and hopes, and joys of the Christian
reflect Christ's image, and answer to the life that gives them birth
and being, and furnishes them with growth, and strength, and vigor.

Again, much honor is conferred upon the soul by the tokens and

mementoes of IMMANUEL'S love, as they are enumerated in the text of
Bunyan, and explained in the margin of the original work. For
example, he enumerates the ring, which he interprets as "a token of
marriage;" and a gold chain, which is "a token of *honor;*" and a brace-
let, which is intended to imply "a token of *beauty;*" and a white stone,
which, as in the promise to the Church of Pergamos, indicates "a
token of *pardon.*"

Mr. God's-Peace.—The last of this great series of gifts was in the
appointment of a new officer over the town—Mr. GOD'S-PEACE. This
principle pervades all, and rules over all, in the soul of the believer.
Its origin is from heaven. It is that peace of God shed abroad in the
heart which blesses and sanctifies the whole man—body, soul, and
spirit; and, under its genial sway, all faith, and hope, and love, and
joy, are multiplied; the thoughts are joyous, the feelings happy, and
the soul at peace!

All that summer.—Well does Bunyan call this the summer-tide of
the soul—a season of clear sunshine and bright prospect; while the
soul enjoys the gifts and graces of the Spirit, and realizes the sweet,
peaceful presence of IMMANUEL. Satan is now driven far away; his
agents lurk and hide in exile; the health of the soul is a saving
health; its joys are great; its privileges large; its hope, and faith,
and love are multiplied; and all the blessed fruits of the Spirit
abound. It is indeed the summer-time of the soul, when the good
seed sown puts forth its varied blossoms, and the bright sunshine
ripens, with its genial warmth, the rich fruits. How sad to think
that any winter's storm should devastate so fair a scene!

CHAPTER IX

DANGER TO MANSOUL

OUTLINE OF CHAPTER IX.—Mr. Carnal-Security.—His Pedigree and Character.—Deceives Mansoul.—Love waxes cold.—The offended Prince withdraws his Presence.—The Consequences to Mansoul.—Mr. Godly-Fear arouses Mansoul to its Danger and its Duty.—Carnal-Security destroyed.—Mansoul seeks, but finds not.—A Day of Darkness.—A solemn Sabbath.—Conscience thunders.—Sickness in Mansoul.—A Fast proclaimed.—Boanerges preaches.—Petition to Immanuel.—No Answer.

Mr. Carnal-Security.—In the midst of safety there is danger. There are elements of strife in the most peaceful scene; and now we have to record a new beginning of sorrows. We have just been contemplating the renewed condition of the soul—chartered, enfranchised, and invested with peculiar rights and privileges; and all these accompanied by timely cautions and admonitions. The soul is at rest and peace, rejoicing in God its Savior, basking in the sunshine of the Prince's favor, and spending its summer-time of joy and gladness. The whole firmament is filled with light; and all seems "set fair," without a prospect of change or drawback.

And yet, at this hopeful crisis, the scene changes again. The soul, lacking watchfulness, and heeding not the timely cautions of the Prince, permits the principle of Carnal Security to spring up. This is a corrupt element of our carnal nature, the offspring of spiritual carelessness and self-conceit. This principle is the result of the fallen nature of man—the consequence of pride, self-sufficiency, and self-righteousness, tending to the grievous decline and downfall of the soul's spiritual health.

"Woe to them that are at ease in Sion," is an expression of the danger that now besets the soul. And this after such large and liberal gifts of God! "What could have been done more to my vineyard, that I have not done in it? Wherefore, when I looked that it should bring forth grapes, brought it forth wild grapes?" Isaiah 5:4.

Carnal-Security is a time-serving principle, conforming itself to all circumstances. It had served under DIABOLUS, and now professes to serve the King in the day of the renewal. On either side, and under any circumstances, the element of Carnal-Security is fraught with danger to the soul. It is a snare to many, who rest on their oars when they ought to be pulling hard against the stream; who sheathe the sword when they ought to be waging a manly warfare; and who sleep a deep slumber of fancied security when the enemy is at their very gates. "And while men slept, the enemy came!"

The giving heed to this spirit of Carnal-Security causes the Captains to be grieved—the graces of the soul to be offended. Accordingly, the love of the soul is chilled; its need of Christ is less experienced and felt. Intercourse with Christ is therefore interrupted; the visits of IMMANUEL are less frequent; and, in process of time, Jesus prepares to withdraw himself from the soul. There is now no open manifestation of Christ the Savior, no friendliness; a spirit of estrangement springs up; and, at last, IMMANUEL arises, and departs from the habitation of the heart.

And this departure is straightway followed by a second woe: IMMANUEL takes counsel with the indwelling SPIRIT; and the Spirit, striving with man, but quite unheeded, is also grieved, and removes his habitation from the dwelling-place of the soul.

In seasons of international misunderstanding, and upon an open declaration of war, the representatives of the belligerent powers are recalled to their respective courts. And even so is it in the case of the soul's disobedience—in the outbreak of mutiny and breach of faith towards Christ. The Son and the Spirit are alike recalled; and, accordingly, both of these forsake the soul. And no sooner have they departed, than GOD'S-PEACE lays down his commission, and he too is gone! And now is the soul in a state of downfall much to be deplored. From a state of unconcern and callous self-security, the transition is immediate—to the abandonment of the soul to frivolity, and feasting, and sin.

The Antinomian spirit of fancied security is here pointed out and condemned—that spirit of evil which whispers to some men thoughts of living as they list and of doing as they like, sheltering themselves all the time under the security of the holy covenant of God. This spirit—so carelessly secure and so recklessly unconcerned—is the cause of grievous downfall to many, who flatter themselves that God's covenant of peace and the assurance of salvation will suffice to cover their heads in the day of self-imposed danger. This is a grievous error, and it has proved fatal to many. To the best and holiest of men, the dearest and best beloved children of God, the elect according to his purpose, is the word of this admonition spoken—"Thou standest by faith. Be not high-minded, but fear," Romans 11:20.

Mr. Godly-Fear.—Amid this blank desolation of the soul, there yet remained one bond of former and better days—in the principle of GODLY-FEAR. The renewed soul, once born again and made the property of Christ by a covenant with God, must ever have at least one binding link that still unites it, though it may be but feebly, to Christ. Hence the command to the Church of Sardis—"Strengthen the things which remain, that are ready to die," Revelation 3:2.

The principle of Godly Fear in the soul is not so high or so hallowed a principle as that of God's Peace, which has just departed and gone. But Godly Fear is now the representative of "the things that remain;" and well and boldly does "the fear of God" in man reprove the erring soul and rebuke the sinner in the decline of his faith, and hope, and love. The words of Godly Fear are like the arrows of conviction in the soul. It calls to remembrance the days of old; it openly reproaches the spirit of Carnal Security; it appeals to the conscience and experience of man, to tell how real is the decline of his joy, and peace, and blessedness, and sets before the soul the contrast between its present low, degraded, and desolate condition, and its former state when IMMANUEL and the SPIRIT reigned within, as the saving and sanctifying principles of the man of God.

By these admonitions of Godly Fear, the Conscience is aroused. Yes, even "the subordinate preacher" has been asleep; his warning voice silenced; and himself under the influence of the charmer! The spirit of false security lulls even the conscience to an untimely sleep; and it must needs be awaked. And it awakes at the call of Godly Fear; but, alas! only to find Christ and the Spirit gone! Then is the Conscience horribly afraid, and, awaking from its guilty sleep, in all the freshness of its first alarm, it communicates all its worst fears to the apprehensions of the soul.

When the fear of God and an awakened Conscience revive in the soul in the day of man's unfaithfulness and decline of love, then do they raise great storms of conviction, and make the soul to realize what it has lost by the departure of its Prince and Savior. It is under such circumstances of the soul that the spirit of Carnal Security is sought out, and found, and utterly destroyed. Fear breaks the charm of security, and causes the soul, in all its bitterness, to say—

"Where is the blessedness I knew
When first I saw the Lord?
Where is the soul-refreshing view
Of Jesus and his Word?"*

A day gloomy and dark.—It is not, however, all sunshine yet; the past is not thus easily restored; and the soul must yet pass many days of gloom and sadness ere its former peace shall be recovered. The soul is sorely wounded by its transgression, and has lost its evidence; Christ is no longer indwelling there. It is easier to drive him out than to fetch him back again; easier to wound than to heal. The heart now seeks the Spirit and the Son, but they will not hear; and the soul is left all-desolate, the victim of its own repinings.

Meanwhile Conscience thunders in the ears of the Soul. Its duty now is that of preacher and adviser to Mansoul, and it has itself been just awakened to a sense of duty neglected, and danger and loss incurred. And what a sermon he preaches, and with how terrible a voice! That Sabbath-day was a day of stormy words, agitating thoughts, and strong convictions—a day of earnest preaching, and of powerful pleading, arousing the whole man to a sense of his sin, and to a consciousness of his danger.

Conscience, thus awakened and aroused to duty, is as the voice of God within us. It is the index finger of truth, rightly set, and pointing, as the needle to the pole, to the one fixed point of settled truth and safety. It is as the true physician, who probes, however painfully, to the deepest core of the disease. It is as the lighthouse, established upon a rock, steadfast amid the troubled waves, at the same time shedding a lustre over the dark waters, and giving timely warning of existing danger. It is as the rudder of the vessel, steering the mariner in a direct course to the haven where he would be. It is a law written on the heart, restraining from sin; not only a terror to evildoers, but also a praise to them that do well. It is an indwelling Providence, about our bed, and about our path, and spying out all our ways. It is a rod of discipline; the searching medicine of the soul; a messenger that will not cease to scourge until its work is done. It is a hard matter to resist this goad of conscience, driving us whither we must go.

And (as often is the case) these alarms of Conscience—these terrors of a troubled mind, are followed by sickness of body and (worse than all) by sickness of mind—"The whole head is sick, the whole

---

*William Cowper, *O for a Closer Walk with God*, 1772.

heart is faint." This also is a dispensation of God; it lays the body low, it subdues the passions, it makes man thoughtful, and renders him more susceptible of impressions for good. This is a day of the soul's weariness—"vexation of spirit." It is tossed about upon a sea of trouble, and finds no rest. The bow of the mighty is unstrung, and the strength of the strong ones is as weakness. The result is, "pale faces"—fear, and alarm, and dread hath covered them; "weak hands"—the working power of the Christian man declines; "feeble knees"—the might of prayer is turned to nought; "and staggering men"—no consistency or strength, no walking uprightly, no steady, onward progress of the soul to God.

And, as may well be imagined, the white garment could not but be soiled, rent, and spotted by this untoward leaning to earth, and by this groveling in earthly things. And so the robe of righteousness doth also but ill-befit the wearer when he walks in the way of ungodliness. Ill-fitted, soiled, and torn is the state of the Christian's spiritual dress when he strays in the bye-paths of his own devising, and departs from the love, and peace, and law of God.

Under such circumstances as these the soul betakes itself to fasting and humiliation. BOANERGES resumes the severity of his office, and the "son of thunder" tells the awful message of the offended Lord. And all is fear and dread of coming wrath. Still, Godly Fear is the adviser of the soul; and it is well it is so. This is the remnant of grace, the residue of the Spirit; and its tendency is to "strengthen the things which remain, that are ready to die."

Send an humble petition.—After humiliation is prayer; and the soul appeals to its absent Prince. But the prayer is neither received nor answered. The soul is now passing through another season of unavailing prayer. It is a day of weeping and mourning, and humiliation in sackcloth and ashes. And the soul prays, and prays again; for the principle of Godly Fear would have men "always to pray." The soul is in hourly communication with the Prince; and yet there is no message of peace nor any to answer! Well does Bunyan suggest in the margin this admonitory reflection—"See what is the work of a backsliding saint awakened!"

God tries the soul of his disobedient children. It is good for them that they should be tried. It is easy to shake confidence, but not so easy to recover it. And this testing process is most severely felt and experienced when the soul resorts to prayer, and finds its prayers to be unavailing. Full of want, conscious of his manifold need, the soul refusing to be otherwise comforted, the backslider lays himself low in the dust, and "out of the deep" he cries to the Lord; and yet his wants are not supplied, his soul is still alarmed, his faith fails to gain an audience of the King, his prayers reach not the ears of the God of Hosts; his supplications go forth frequent and oft, and laden with the burden of his necessities, but they all return empty into his bosom. In that day of test and trial, the eye of the soul looks out for the hoped-for succors, but sees no help arriving; the ears wait to catch the faint echoes of the expected deliverance, but no sound is borne to the hearing sense; the hand is stretched forth to grasp the long-desired help, but it has grasped the wind! "Who shall deliver me?" is the cry that goes up from the unsatisfied soul.

That reverend Mr. Godly-Fear.—This stern and unflinching adviser of the soul seems to discharge the same office to the erring Christian as EVANGELIST is said to have done to the Pilgrim, as described in the PILGRIM'S PROGRESS. When CHRISTIAN had yielded to the ill-advice of the tempter, and had been led astray to the rugged sides of Sinai, instead of speeding the direct way to the Wicket Gate, then it was that EVANGELIST met him, and "coming up to him with a severe and dreadful countenance, began to reason with him." And his reasonings were harsh, severe, and threatening; and yet, after the admonition, he directed the erring Pilgrim into the way again, and gave him the kiss of peace, and smiled upon him, and bade him Godspeed in his journey. And so now, GODLY-FEAR is, at first, the stern censor of the soul, his voice rebuking the spirit of Carnal-Security, and urging the soul to put it utterly away and out of existence; and yet, by-and-by, he becomes the calm adviser of MANSOUL'S good, encouraging the soul in prayer, urging it to continue its supplication at the throne of grace, and pointing out what are the ways of God in his dealing and discipline with his erring children—a long-suffering God, who beareth long, but doth at last hear, and heed, and grant the request of persistent, patient prayer.

All that long, sharp, cold, and tedious winter.—The former phase of the soul's state, as described at the conclusion of the preceding chapter, was that of a happy "summer," all joy and blessedness. But now it is not so; it is the soul's "winter-time."

This dreary and desolate season of spiritual decline is said to have been "long." Winter is sometimes a prolonged period of desolation; and so the soul's spiritual winter is at times made to be long and weary. "My soul is sore vexed: but thou, O Lord, how long?" Psalm 6:3. "How long wilt thou forget me, O Lord? for ever? how long wilt thou hide thy face from me?" Psalm 13:1.

It was also "sharp." The loss of evidence is a severe loss, and God will have the soul to *feel* it—this sharp, pinching sense of loss and loneliness; like the biting frosts of midwinter, drying, parching, withering, blighting all that the summer-time has developed and brought forth. "All our pleasant things are laid waste," Isaiah 64:11.

And it was "cold." Yes, cold in every way; because all warmth had gone, and a piercing east wind prevailed; the fountains of love were sealed, and the streams restrained. Mansoul basked not in the warm sunshine of God's countenance; her heart was cold, her love cold—all was chill in the ice of a dead wintertime.

And it was, moreover, "tedious." All such alternations, from high privilege to the withdrawal of our pleasant things, are sure to be unenjoyable, and therefore tedious. Long are the days of sorrow, and tedious the nights of pain.

Such is the probation and discipline of the soul; and this may yet continue for many days. It is the season of the hiding of the face of Jesus, the withdrawing of his Spirit, when the soul is without cheer or comfort, because it is without Christ. Dark and dreary, indeed, are all such seasons to the soul. "Wherefore let him that thinketh he standeth take heed lest he fall!"

CHAPTER X

A DIABOLONIAN PLOT

OUTLINE OF CHAPTER X.—The Lurking Diabolonians revive in Mansoul.—Mr. Mischief.—A Council held.—Letter to Diabolus.—The Bearer of the Letter, Mr. Profane.—Joy in Hell.—The Answer of Diabolus.—Counsel of Mr. Deceit.—A Cunning Expedient devised.—Diabolonians in Disguise.—Report to Diabolus.—A Council of Devils.—Impatience of Diabolus.—Threatened Assault.—The Army of Terrible Doubters.—Feeble Petition to the Prince; but "Immanuel was gone!"

Many of the old Diabolonians.—The offspring of Mansoul is now manifold. Many of the better principles have been wedded to those of the baser sort. The result is that evil is propagated, and sin is multiplied. The "works of the flesh" (Galatians 5:19) abound; while the "fruits of the Spirit" (Galatians 5:22) are diminished and brought low. Thus, within the soul, sins are found in family groups—some older, some younger; some larger, some smaller; some parents, some offspring. There is a parentage and pedigree of sin, and a strong family likeness pervading all the members. There is a heraldry of sin, with its dark family escutcheon, crossed with many a bar of spiritual bastardy. Sin is the aged parent of the past, stretching her protracted age even to the present, and still prolific of a deadly progeny. "When lust hath conceived, it bringeth forth sin: and sin, when it is finished, bringeth forth death." This lineal continuity is not yet exhausted in the soul; it breeds its offspring still. This has been the great danger of the soul, from the first day of its transgression even until now.

Accordingly, we have found that one of the strictest and most oft repeated charges to the soul had been, that the Diabolonians should be utterly destroyed. Their continuance in the soul is but the prolific seed of future mischief, lurking for a season in the soil, waiting for time, circumstance, and opportunity to develop their growth and increase. To this charge the soul does not give sufficient heed; it trifles with its safety, and ere long loses its evidence. This phase of spiritual experience answers to that of the Pilgrim, when he slept where he ought not, and lost the roll of his parchment, the evidence of his adoption, and with difficulty recovered it.

It is a dark day for the soul when the lurking power of Satan revives, and meditates evil to the soul's health and peace. The uncertainty of the renewed man, after trifling with Divine grace, is Satan's chosen opportunity, when he comes forth more boldly than before, seduces the soul into sin, and reduces it to deeper bondage day by day. This is the soul's probation: it had received command to destroy the Diabolonians, but they are not destroyed. They live— and live for mischief. When the soul dallies with temptation, reposing on the lap of its spiritual Delilah, it fails to fight the good fight of faith; all carnal things revive and grow, while the things of the Spirit decline and die.

And this probation may continue long. A single act of unfaithfulness may bring forth years of sorrow. Such is the experience of many a Christian man who has trifled with his old enemy—sin. How many weary steps had the Pilgrim to retrace ere he recovered his lost parchment! how many weary days were spent in seeking back to the path of the pilgrimage from Doubting Castle! how many years of distress and anguish did Bunyan himself endure, while bereft of light, and joy, and comfort! This is ever the chosen time of Satan's temptation—when Christ has departed from the soul. So the Diabolonians once more take heart, and meditate the re-capture of the whole man.

So they met together.—A council is held; the trysting-place is the house of Mr. MISCHIEF, one rightly so named, for his influence involves mischief to the hopes, mischief to the joys, mischief to the peace, mischief to the evidence of the soul. A crafty and cunning expedient is devised—that the Diabolonian principles are to offer themselves as servants of the spiritual nature; that is, the carnal and sinful desires of the flesh are to enter into the service of the better feelings of the soul, so as to corrupt the affections, to chequer the joys, to forfeit the hopes, and, if possible, to destroy the life, and health, and being of the once man of God. There is great and vital danger in any incorporation of evil with good. Even as hired servants, the Diabolonian principles are dangerous. The evil soon gains the mastery, and tramples the good under its feet.

So a letter was framed.—But not without communication with their master do these evil principles propound their plans. The evil heart takes council of Satan, and corresponds with its master, to the great injury of the soul. So a letter is sent. This is the leaning of the carnal mind to Satan; it reports the decline of religion in the heart; it tells how the Prince has departed, and how the soul is reduced to a state of utter weakness and want.

The occasion of this "letter" suggests a few words by way of explanation: the soul is still the property of Christ, but its first love has grown cold, and its affections have declined from the dominion of Christ. There is a revival of the evil nature, indicated by the consultation of certain carnal principles, that now seek to regain their former mastery. These carnal principles are the medium of the soul's communication with the Evil One. They have been kept down, mortified, restrained, under the superior regimen and discipline of the soul; but now the reins are relaxed, and the evil nature in proportion is released; and, seizing its opportunity, it instantly springs back, as a bow unstrung, and with its recovered energy it begins to tell against the soul. Now is it that the rising thoughts seek after Satan, the old desires long after his loose rein, and the carnal nature holds direct intercourse with hell. When evil thought thus answers to the thought of evil, and carnal desires answer to the desires of the flesh, and the corrupt nature is in communion with the powers of darkness, the spiritual health is, indeed, brought very low.

And not only the occasion of the "letter," but also the purport of the communication demands attention. The evil nature addresses Satan as its rightful liege lord, as the very father of its being—"Ye are of your father the devil, and the lusts of your father ye will do," John 8:44. The corrupt principles acknowledge that for some time past they have not felt at home in Mansoul; nor indeed can sin ever feel itself welcome in a heart possessed of an indwelling Christ. Yet do these corruptions of the "old man" linger and lurk in the hiding-places of the flesh and spirit, waiting for an opportunity; and such an opportunity seems now to have been granted; and they seek to take advantage of the occasion to recover their lost dominion. The chief hopes of the evil nature are based upon the following circumstances—that IMMANUEL has departed; that the prayers and petitions of the soul seem no longer to be regarded; and that a sore sickness and debility has spread itself over all the holier principles, thoughts, and feelings, to the great discomfort of the soul. Conscience rebukes the backslider; and his sin-sickness weakens him, and lays him low. All this is duly reported to their master by the thoughts of the evil heart of unbelief, and form the burden of the message of the soul to Satan.

Mr. Profane.—The bearer of the letter—Mr. PROFANE—indicates that spirit in man that sets at nought things Divine, and urges the soul to direct communication with the Evil One. Every evil thought or desire in the heart is a medium of communication with Satan; for in entertaining such, we consult his pleasure, and, as it were, seek counsel at his lips.

Cerberus, the Porter.—It is not often that Bunyan introduces into his writings any words or names from the heathen classics. Indeed, he seems rather to avoid introducing any allusions that might lead his readers to suppose him to have been familiar with Latin and Greek authors. In the second part of the PILGRIM'S PROGRESS, where he records in Latin the prescription of the physician, Dr. SKILL, he takes care, by reason of his unassuming humility, to state in a side-note, "The Latin I borrow." In the HOLY WAR, however, he seems to exercise more freedom in this respect. For example, he gives the name of Tisiphone (one of the fabled furies) to the person who, in the first assault upon Mansoul, slew Captain RESISTANCE. He also freely applies the names of the other furies of classic story, Alecto and Megaera, to persons and things in the present Allegory—sometimes giving the names to devils in the council of hell, and sometimes calling the strongholds of DIABOLUS by those appellations, as we shall find in a subsequent part of the story.

So here, the name of CERBERUS is borrowed from the heathen poets and other writers, who gave that name to the fabled dog of Tartarus, the keeper of the gate of the infernal region. This dog was said to have had three heads, and to have kept watch and ward over the gates of the abyss, that no lost soul should ever be permitted to pass again through those dread portals of the pit. The name is here appropriately applied to the sentinel door-keeper of the den of DIABOLUS.

Dead-man's bell should be rung for joy.—There is joy in heaven over one sinner that repents and turns to God; and so there is joy in hell over one soul that turns back from its repentance, and seeks counsel at the lips of the destroyer. The joy of hell, whither, it is said, "joy ne'er comes, that comes to all," is for the loss, or hoped-for loss, of souls—lost to Christ and gained to Satan. The first overtures of such backsliding souls are welcome to the ears of hell, and infuse a ray of joy even into the misery of the damned.

Thus hell rejoices, and sends back its answer to the soul. The counsel of Satan ever is—to weaken the soul more and more. And there are many ways to accomplish this; in some, by a loose and wicked life; in others, by doubt and despair; and in others, by pride and self-conceit. By each and all of these means does Satan accomplish his work—according as he discovers the weak point in each of his tempted victims. And, to ascertain this weak point, Satan makes inquiry of the soul itself, being ready to accept its own way, to yield to its own desire, and to pander to its own wishes. Satan does not dictate to the soul the ways and means of destruction, but accepts the soul's own method, as its bent, or inclination, or besetting sin marks out. Well does Bunyan introduce in a side-note this admonition—"Take heed, Mansoul!"

It is a fearful thing to open negotiations with Satan; and, as surely as any Diabolonian power awakes, a way of communication is instantly opened with the powers of hell, and Satan straightway answers. It is easy to conjure up the spirits of the deep; easy to awake the carnal thought; easy to develop a whole train of evil thoughts, extending to evil desires, and working out in open deeds of sin. These influences of the corrupt and carnal nature are the natural allies of Satan in the heart; and when there is opportunity, there is no lack of intercourse with the power of evil. And these are greatly encouraged by their master; for he promises that they shall yet again be lords, and have dominion over the soul. This full, free, and unrestricted power is the desire of the evil nature still lurking in the inner man. Grace, indeed, restrains it; grace subdues it; for grace still reigneth in the heart, which Christ has purchased and possessed, albeit he is now absent. Oh, let this grace abound and be multiplied in this the perilous season of the soul!

> "Only do not Thou forsake me;
> Oh, be Thou for ever near!"

How they might complete their design.—Encouraged by the prompt answer of their chief, the evil principles of the soul wax more presumptuous, and instantly proceed to give effect to the suggestions of Satan. And to the more complete accomplishment of their purpose, the conspirators determine to maintain the secrecy of their design. The two natures are distinct, and still opposed; and therefore it is to the interest of the carnal nature to work secretly, lest it should prematurely disclose its plans, and awake the spiritual nature to vigilance and defense. How often do men enact these conspiracies against the soul, in the secret thoughts of the heart! When the power of sin revives, and the heart holds counsel with evil, the craft and subtlety of Satan suggests secrecy—the blinding of the conscience, the bribing of the will, the tampering with the power of the understanding. And the chief agent in this secret process is here rightly named DECEIT. "The deceived heart" is that which is most likely to be kept in ignorance of the devices of Satan. The period of man's ignorance is the period of Satan's progress; the season of the untimely sleep of the servants is the season of the sowing of the tares among the good seed. "An enemy hath done this!"

Proffer themselves for servants.—How wily was this plot; and how true to the letter of our own experience of life and the world! If the nature of the temptation repels us, does it not often happen that a change of name sufficiently disguises the evil, so that we more readily fall into it? We sometimes consult the *name* more than the *nature* of particular temptations; and thus the hellish plot succeeds.

Here three notable Diabolonians disguise themselves by change of dress and change of name, and, under this mask, are received into the service of the better principles of the soul. The Mind, and the Will, and even Godly Fear, are tampered with, and fall into the snare. Vices are harbored under the name and garb of virtues; and thus, at the counsel of Deceit, man is deceived.

All this is true in our experience; and this phase of the Allegory supplies another exquisite proof of Bunyan's thorough knowledge of human nature, and of the ways of men. For example—

There is many a man who would not permit himself to be called a "covetous" man, and who would himself call "covetousness" a sin, who is, nevertheless, setting his heart upon his gain, under pretext of making proper provision for his family. It is the very spirit of covetousness, all the time; but he calls it by the more harmless but more seductive name of Prudent-Thrift. It is this setting of the heart's affection upon worldly wealth and earthly gain that gives the point to the words of our blessed Lord when he said, "How hardly shall they that have riches enter into the kingdom of God"— a sentiment which he immediately afterwards interprets to mean, "How hard is it for them that *trust in riches* to enter into the kingdom of God," Mark 10:23–24.

There is another, who would repel the charge of "anger;" but yet his spirit may be soured by prejudice and embittered by partiality; and in his very anger he may persecute, or betray, or even burn you. He calls it "Good-Zeal;" but it is the spirit of "anger" notwithstanding, and a sin. Sir Everard Digby, one of the conspirators in the Gunpow- der Treason, wrote thus to his wife, after his condemnation:—"If I had thought there had been the least sin in the plot, I would not have been of it for all the world; and no other cause drew me to hazard my fortune and life but *zeal* to God's religion." (Hume's History, chapter 46) It is respecting this deceptive sin that Jesus spake, when he said—"Yea, the time cometh, that whosoever killeth you will think that he doeth God service," John 16:2.

And there is yet another, who would avoid open and presumptuous sins, and yet he introduces into his house, under the milder name of Harmless-Mirth, the very essence of the spirit of worldly pleasure, and so mingles the world with religion as to bring the soul into bondage and captivity. It behoves the best of us to guard diligently against the encroachment of the world and of pleasure upon the holy places of the soul; and more especially in this age, in which worldly pleasures incline so very near to ungodliness and sin. There are but few worldly pleasures that are wholly innocent, and but little worldly "mirth" that can be called altogether "harmless."

A market-day would be best.—It would be well to observe that the time chosen for practicing this deception on the soul was during the busy engagements of the world, under high pressure of worldly business, appropriately called here a "market-day." When the mind, and the will, and even the fear of God in man, are cumbered with much worldly business, it is a season that demands much watchfulness. The work-time of the body—the season of anxious care and business—may be the time of greatest damage to the soul. While the man of business is hoarding up money, driving a prosperous trade, making haste to be rich, and encompassed with the cares of this life, he may be most of all exposed to the craft and subtlety of the "Diabolonian Plot." It was after the purchase of the farm, the merchandise, and the yoke of oxen, that the invited guests "began with one consent to make excuse."

We are accustomed to regard the "days of Lot" as a season of intense wickedness and impiety; and no doubt those days were intensely corrupt, and far gone in ungodliness and sin. But when our blessed Lord would describe the character of that age, and the sin of that generation, he draws no darker picture than what is true of every age, and singularly applies to our own day— detailing a catalogue, not of the grosser sins committed against God and man, but an enumeration of the daily round of worldly business—"They did eat, they drank, they bought, they sold, they planted, they builded." And though we all know that to eat and drink, and buy and sell, and plant and build, are not in themselves acts of sin, yet we also know that, somehow, it was in the midst of these engagements, and while wrapped up in them, that "it rained fire and brimstone from heaven, and destroyed them all," Luke 17:28–29. This is a solemn admonition to those who are, however necessarily, lawfully, or even laudably, connected with the world and the things of the world, that they make not these the occasion of the flesh, the cause of forgetfulness of God, and the reason of their decline of faith and love. It needs not that a man should wax openly profane; nor that he be the unfaithful steward, who wasted his master's substance; nor the prodigal who squandered his means in riotous living. That a man should permit his ordinary business to gain the mastery over him, to the exclusion of the thoughts of God, and Christ, and heaven—*this* sufficeth for condemnation!

Another letter to Diabolus.—A second letter addressed to DIABOLUS reports progress, and communicates the choice of measures for the re-taking of the soul. The carnal nature in man ever acts in concert with its master, Satan; and although Satan leaves the erring soul very much to its own devices, still the carnal mind is *his* nature in man, and it does his bidding, and ever seeks instruction at his mouth.

The plot now thickens: partial success has already attended past efforts. The downfall of the soul is too truly answering to the designs of Satan. The Mind has been induced to take into its service the evil principle of "covetousness," and, ere long, the servant rules the master. The Will has given way to worldly "mirth," and has been led on to degradation far deeper than that word of itself implies, and finds himself at last a slave of lust, given over to wantonness and presumptuous sin. All this is the ripening of the plot; and, as it ripens, it is more and more helpful to the designs of the evil nature. It is, in fact, the story of "the Flatterer" told over again, as in the PILGRIM'S PROGRESS—"a man, black of flesh, but covered with a very light robe;" but he beckoned them away from the path of safety, by the *scarcely perceptible divergence* of the road of danger, and at last enclosed them in his net. And, now that they have discovered their mistake, they are reminded of the advice given them to "beware of the Flatterer," and could then but give answer—"Yes, but we did not imagine that this fine-spoken man was he!"

The secret conclave next takes counsel respecting the suggestions of Satan, as to the best way to take the soul. The choice ultimately was to employ the weapon of Doubt and Desperation, as being the best calculated to succeed in the present case:—"We think that an army of doubters may be most likely to attack and overcome the town of Mansoul."

This opens up the sequel of the HOLY WAR in its concluding stages. Decline of faith and love is followed by soul-sickness; lack of watchfulness has exposed the soul to evil thoughts and evil deeds; these have gradually been gaining the mastery, and leading the soul into captivity. Meanwhile, the unconcern of man blinds his eyes to the onward progress of the evil nature. The scheme is still a secret conspiracy, not yet fully disclosed to the better nature; and now it is to the interest of Satan to reduce the soul to a state of sin, so that when it awakes to the reality of its condition, it may be seized with a spirit of despair, and resign all hope of renewal of pardon and acceptance.

In a Sad and Woeful Case.—All the symptoms show a rapid decline of the once joy and sunshine of the soul, a far-gone decay of its former strength and vigor, and the near setting of the light of its glory. The soul is gradually becoming more and more conscious of its vileness and degradation—more and more hopeless as to the return of its departed Lord, or the renewal of his favor. The once strong man has slept a deep unhallowed sleep, and now awakes to find the power of the Philistines upon him, and himself a helpless victim in their hands. What was his past glory then but condemnation? What, that he had once rent a lion by the way as he would have rent a kid? What, that he had upheaved the ponderous gates of Gaza, bar and all, and carried them to the hill-top? What, that when the Philistines shouted against him at the rock Etam, the spirit of the Lord came mightily upon him, and the cords upon his arms became as flax that is burned with fire, and "with the jaw-bone of an ass, heaps upon heaps, with the jaw of an ass he had slain a thousand men?" By trifling with the gift of his great strength, by abusing the grace given unto him, by "taking fire into his bosom," by indulging the spirit of carnal security, he smarted for his sin, and was bereaved of strength, and liberty, and light, and joy, and peace in one day. And so, what are all the past experiences of the soul, the blessed memories of better days, the feasts and visits of IMMANUEL, the tokens of his love, the badges of his favor, the presents from his table— what, but the greater cause for the writing of "Ichabod" upon her dismantled walls—"the glory is departed!"

"Beware! The Israelite of old, who tore
    The lion in his path—when, poor and blind,
He saw the blessed light of heaven no more.
    Shorn of his noble strength, and forced to grind
In prison, and at last led forth to be
A pander to Philistine revelry!"

Consulted what Answer to Return.—There is thought and fore-thought in hell; craft and subtlety in Satan. Many minds and manifold devices seem to be in operation in the deep places of the pit. Satan is a wily general, who weighs and counter-weighs his plans before he gives them ultimate effect. A very remarkable and suggestive description of this is here recorded by Bunyan, revealing the workings of the Satanic mind, the agonies of the King of hell while, as it were, travailing in birth, he brings forth the most deadly designs against the soul. In this deliberation, cautious counsels are delivered; and we are taught this great truth, that Satan fears and respects man's extra vigilance, and that, if man does not watch and be sober, Satan is satisfied that "*any day* will do" for the assault.

Their Cumber in Business.—When man is, with the heart, serving Mammon, he cannot be serving Christ. Accordingly, the Diabolonian opportunity would seem to fall most likely on a market day. Yet the state of the soul, as described in this phase of its experience, was not a state of utter abandonment to sin, or of a determined condition of unwatchfulness. The soul, still possessed of some small remnant of grace, would take alarm upon a known emergency; and is, perhaps, not so far gone in its decline of faith and love, as to omit to take precautions on special occasions. Hence the wily suggestions of LUCIFER, in the Diabolonian counsel, by which Bunyan would have us to understand somewhat of the devices of Satan, in well measuring his ground, and maturing his plans, and making provision against the possible vigilance of the soul.

Inquire about it of Mr. Profane.—Everything seems to depend on man's spirit of watchfulness and prayer. Vigilance is on the look-out for threatened or approaching danger, and Prayer calls in the aid of the King in time of need. Accordingly, the council of hell pauses for a moment to make inquiry as to the spirit of Mansoul in these respects. The Naughtiness of Man (PROFANE) is the informant on this occasion, and it reports nothing good respecting Mansoul, with this one exception of prayer. PROFANE reports an evident decline of faith and love, the departure of the Lord, and, though Mansoul prays, yet that there is no improvement or reformation of life; but still he cannot deny that Mansoul is given to prayer.

Afraid of their Petitioning.—Still Mansoul prays, and this is what most discourages DIABOLUS. True, the prayer was unheeded and unanswered, but still it was *prayer.* "Behold, he prayeth!" Yea, the prayer was even weak and feeble, but still it was *prayer.* How true are the words of Montgomery's beautiful hymn!

> "And Satan trembles when he sees
> The *weakest* saint upon his knees."

That the soul prays at all at such a crisis of its forlorn hope is owing altogether to the still abiding of GODLY-FEAR in the heart. He urges the soul ever on to prayer—"always to pray, and not to faint." It is the great experiment of remaining faith and fear—prayer to the offended Prince.

Two or three Diabolonians.—And yet another thought occurs, suggested by the great APOLLYON, to go fair and softly, and allow the evil nature to work out its own results, making the soul more sinful and corrupt. A few traitors within the camp, enemies disguised as friends, yea, receiving sustenance and pay as servants, are a thousand times more hurtful than an open armament or expedition from without. The sins that are prompted from within render the soul consciously responsible, and it blames itself, and ofttimes is seized by the spirit of despair, and says, "I will be yet more vile." This method would seem also to be the more natural out-working of the evil nature, and better calculated to overwhelm the soul in condemnation than a more violent assault of Satan and his legion; for, the more sinful a man becomes, the weaker he grows. Committed sin is one of the greatest allies of the Wicked One; it weakens the spirit of resistance, offends the conscience, hurts the soul, and robs man of his hope in the promises of God. The aim and design of Satan is to make the sinner so sinful as that God should finally and for ever withdraw his presence, and therewith all the things that belong to God—his Word and his ministers, the holy thoughts and virtues of the soul. Then, indeed, would *all* be gone!

But this would be a work of time; and meanwhile, his spirit of impatience will not permit the great DIABOLUS to wait; and here occurs a grand and eloquent description of that terrible wrath of the roaring lion, hungering and thirsting after souls. He cannot wait—he has hungered and thirsted long enough, and can refrain no longer—"My furious gorge, and empty paunch, so lusteth after a repossession of my famous town of Mansoul, that whatever comes out, I can wait no longer!"

The word of DIABOLUS is omnipotent in hell, and accordingly, on this occasion, it is promptly obeyed. The meaning is, that Satan's impetuous wrath—his hunger and thirst for souls—sometimes causes him to refuse more wily council, that would be more adapted to the destruction of the soul. There are times, indeed, when Satan outwits himself by his own rapacity and eagerness: like the lion of the forest, which sometimes, in a moment of rapacious hunger, overleaps his prey. So now, the more wily counsels are abandoned, and a fierce assault is decided on, by which it is designed to subjugate the soul, and to bring it finally and for ever under the power of hell.

An Army of Terrible Doubters.—Here commences the inauguration of that terrible army of doubt, which continues to harass the soul, more or less, even to the end. This is an interesting—a painfully interesting—phase of the soul's oft-chequered history. For now the devices of Satan are designed against the few remaining hopes and joys of Mansoul; and a dark and terrible night of anguish is about, for a time at least, to settle upon the spirit of the man, whose spiritual history is here described.

We must not omit to mention here that this phase of the allegory not only opens up the sequel of the HOLY WAR, but also illustrates that arrow of Satan's quiver, which was ever the most powerful against Bunyan himself—the weapon of doubt. Some of us might be more exposed to the assault of pride; others might yield more easily to the wanton and vain spirit; but Bunyan seems ever to have fallen most easily under the power of doubt and desperation. He has, therefore, very naturally thrown this part of his Allegory in the direction of his own experience; and, as he had done in the PILGRIM'S PROGRESS, so now he speaks of himself and of his own fierce struggles with the Wicked One.

Thus, in the PILGRIM'S PROGRESS, we read of the Slough of Despond, and of Doubting Castle and Giant Despair; and even at the last, in the fords of the river, his doubts and fears got the better of his hopes and joys, and had well nigh drowned him in the depths. So also, in his "Grace Abounding," which is his own personal biography, he tells the awful story of his oft-recurring seasons of doubt and dark despair. And so now, in the HOLY WAR, he writes the Allegory in the light of his own personal experience; and, accordingly, lays stress on *this* particular weapon of the Wicked One, as the chosen engine for the renewed assault upon the soul.

Let us, then, in anticipation of the raising of this terrible army, contemplate the purport and meaning of this phase of the soul's experience.

Of doubts in general we may say, with Lord Bacon, "Suspicions are among thoughts as bats among birds: they come out in the twilight." Doubts arise in the dark seasons of the soul, and during the darkness they alarm and terrify the conscience. Doubt is the child of little knowledge—therefore, let it know more; it is the twilight of the soul—then, let the sun arise, and dispel the gloom; it sees through a glass darkly, not with open face—so, open wide the door, and boldly confront the dark and lowering foe, and bid him to begone!

Ignorance of God and of Christ, and of the comforts of the Spirit, is calculated to promote doubt; knowledge of God and Christ and the Spirit dissipates doubt. During this dark season the soul sees no light, because it is shut up, and the windows of the soul are closed and barred against the entrance of light. These doubts are ofttimes like the ghosts we read of; they come out at midnight, but when they hear the cock crowing, and catch the sharp biting air of the morning, when honest folk go forth to labor, they are chased away to their hiding-places. Doubt is the cloud-land of Christians, the suburbs of the experience of many, only needing the sun to shine in its clear noon-day power and glory to dissipate the mists and mysteries of ignorance and doubt. Be bold to touch them with a realizing hand, and they are gone!

A fully detailed account and description of this "terrible army" will be given by Bunyan in the subsequent pages. There we shall be able to read what his master mind—itself so oft exercised by doubt—has to say to his fellow Christians respecting this formidable power of the Evil One. Against Bunyan the armory of hell contained no more potent weapon than this, and with unsparing rigor was it used, making the servant of the Lord to feel how deeply the iron entered into his soul.

From the deep and hungry gorge of hell, from the compassionless bowels of the pit, by the counsel of devils and doomed spirits, at the stern demand of the impatient and infuriate god of the abyss, with the resonant curse of hell as a blessing on the vast enterprise, and with the thousand acclamations of the damned, the decision is arrived at, and the messenger departs with the tidings thereof to the Diabolonians of Mansoul!

And with a thousand welcomes is the messenger received at the hands of Mr. MISCHIEF and his accomplices. There, in the deep recesses of the heart, is this dark conspiracy being advanced to maturity and completeness—the soul unconscious, and all unknowing of its danger. And, as the faith, and fear, and love of Mansoul droop and die, so do the Diabolonian principles wax bold, presumptuous, and wanton. Gradually is the plot unfolding—man in actual communion with hell for his own degradation and ruin, and the pent-up wrath about to burst as the clap of a storm-cloud, and as a deluge of destruction, upon the once pleasant places of the soul.

The Miserable Town of Mansoul.—Ay, miserable indeed! The soul, in its present state, feels its abject wretchedness and its condemnation. It is also sensible of its loss of all evidence, and faith, and hope. The soul cries for help to the Mighty, but he hears it not; it seeks the Lord, but "IMMANUEL is gone!" There is a knowledge of sin, and grief for sin, and yet a fondling of sin in their very bosoms! Now, prayer without effort, repentance without reformation, is but an offence to God. How could the Prince return, while Diabolonians are laid in the very bosom, and to the very heart, of men? It would be an unholy compromise, a half-hearted service, a divided allegiance. The old and the new agree not thus together; it is an unequal yoke. The old piece of cloth is not strong enough to bear the new piece, and the rent is made worse; the old bottles are not adapted for the keeping of the new wine; and if the attempt is made, two evils ensue—the bottles burst and perish, and the wine is spilled and lost. The religion of Christ is not designed merely to mend or repair, but wholly to *renew*. Christ is not only a helper, but a *Savior*—a complete Savior. "All or none" are still the terms of his demand.

The Town diminished greatly.—Lower and deeper, day by day, declines the spiritual health of Mansoul. Meanwhile their loss is Satan's gain, their weakness his strength, their condemnation his glory. All holy thoughts perish at the birth, every spark of heavenly light is quenched at the kindling, or, as Bunyan allegorically puts it, "More than eleven thousand men, women, and children died by the sickness in Mansoul;" meaning by this, as the key in the margin would tell us, the "good thoughts, good conceptions, and good desires" of the soul. Thus far, the Diabolonian plot has prospered, and the sequel remains to be seen.

CHAPTER XI

THE PLOT DISCOVERED

OUTLINE OF CHAPTER XI.—Mr. Prywell discovers the Plot.—
Acquaints the Governors of Mansoul.—Conscience arouses the
Townsmen.—They take Alarm.—Precautions, Preparations, and
Resolutions.—Search for the Lurking Diabolonians.—The Country
of the Doubters.—Spies and Traitors arrested.—The Army of
Doubters.—Their Captains, Standard-bearers, and Escutcheons.—
The March.—The Advance.—Assault upon Ear-Gate.—The Drum of
the Doubters.—Parley with Mansoul.—The Town languishes.

Mr. Prywell.—The Allegory is now ingeniously, and at the same
time experimentally, conducted through the instructive sequel of
the Diabolonian plot. Shall the soul be thus betrayed by treacherous
principles from within, and fall a helpless victim to the power of
Satan and his angels? Is there no overruling power from without, no
wakeful principle within, to apprise the soul of the lurking danger,
which is now, by lapse of time, and by the aid of circumstances,
sufficiently matured for its outward development?

The Great SHADDAI is not unmindful of his once fair heritage; nor is
IMMANUEL utterly dispossessed of Mansoul, though he be absent from
it. The covenant of the Son standeth sure. But Mansoul is on the
point to die, and now has nought of hope, or promise, or dependence,
save in the mysterious covenant of God in Christ. Indeed, the soul
seems almost as though it had sinned away even this; but yet, amid
all its decline, decay, defection, and disobedience, God keeps the
inheritance of his Son, and still "doth he devise means, that his
banished be not expelled from him," 2 Samuel 14:14.

The means adopted are, the awaking of the detective spirit of Mr.
PRYWELL. Hitherto, secrecy had been the seal of the plot. The better
principles of the soul had long been unwakeful, unheeding of the
danger, and, so far, ignorant of the devices of Satan. It was by
stealth, disguise, and secret counsel that the Diabolonians had
proceeded thus far, taking advantage of the soul's slumbering. But
now, the soul awakes, or is awakened, through the agency of one of

the remaining principles of the renewed man—PRYWELL. This is the spirit of self-suspicion and self-examination of the soul—the search-ing, prying spirit, that first tries whether all is right, and then examines what is wrong, and promptly reports the results to the mind, and will, and conscience, and understanding. This principle is here represented as moving to and fro, and going up and down, and searching through and through, all the highways, and by-ways, and thoroughfares, and secret dens of the soul, detecting the thoughts and discovering the intents of the heart, and spying out the hidden collusion of the soul with Satan.

The present decline of Mansoul is owing to its ignorance of its own spiritual state and condition. Now, if we would know ourselves, we must examine ourselves. There is no attainment of self-knowledge without self-examination. And all true and honest self-examination must be conducted in the light of God's Word, and of God's holy law: "Whoso looketh into the perfect law of liberty, and continueth therein, this man shall be blessed in his deed," James 1:25. In the context of this statement of the Apostle, the law of liberty is likened to a "mirror," in which both the "forgetful hearer" and the "not forgetful hearer" look; the one to go away "forgetting what manner of man he was," and the other, as a diligent observer of himself, by self-examination admonished of his failings, going forth *to do* the things that need to be done.

This principle of self-examination is the detector of the heart; it takes stock of the spiritual state, condition, and prospects. Other-wise, a man may be said to live at random, without system, and without object. Self-examination is the gauge of the spiritual expe-rience, measuring either the drought of the parched and thirsty soil or else the depth of the rain-fall of showers of grace and blessings. It is the test of progress in the school of life—the competitive test for promotion and advancement. It is the watch and ward of the inner eye upon the condition of the soul, the sharp look-out upon the inner man. It is the getting to the root, probing to the core, knowing the last, the worst, the uttermost of our state. It is all these; and then to the great IMMANUEL, with a long, lingering look, seeking the defeat of the wiles of Satan, desiring the return of the offended Spirit, and going forth to bid the absent Savior back again. "Arise, O Lord, into thy rest; thou, and the ark of thy strength," Psalm 132:8.

Then, let PRYWELL search the soul, and examine the thoughts. Let a flood of self-knowledge and of Divine light pour into the dark places of Diabolonian conspiracy and design. The more the soul dwells in darkness and ignorance, the more will the revolutionary rabble of sin rise against the throne; and, panic-stricken, the man must flee away, pursued in his flight, and at last lose the mastery. Against secret and unknown dangers, there must be always the element of fear; but in the face of known peril, there may at least be the boldness of the man who has ascertained the measure of the danger.

> "True dignity abides with him alone
> Who, in the silent hour of inward thought,
> Can still suspect, and still revere himself,
> In lowliness of heart."

Self-suspicion tends to keep one watchful. It is the constant irritation that keeps up the healthy circulation. It is the breath that blows upon the waters, and preserves them from stagnation. There is scope enough within ourselves for the daily exercise of this suspicion of self; as some one has said—"When we are alone, we have our thoughts to watch; in our families, our tempers; in company, our tongues; and in religion, our very hearts." It is our safety to probe and examine as we live and move; not, indeed, to see that all is wrong, but (we would fain hope) to discover that all is right.

No sooner has a railway train stopped at a station, than you hear the clatter of hammers upon the wheels. What meaneth this? It is self-suspicion and self-examination. But this diligent and oft-repeated inquiry does not break the wheels, or render you at all unsafe; but, in the result of the trial, proves that all is safe and sound.

Gave the alarm to the town.—This is the work of Conscience, the only teacher that now abides in Mansoul. Self-examination has first to do with the lurking danger; and then, having discovered the peril, its next business is with the Conscience, which is not now, as it once was, merely the recorder or remembrancer of the town; but is possessed of the higher and more responsible office of preacher and adviser of the soul. Accordingly, Conscience rings his bell, awakes the soul, shakes it from its slumber, betakes himself to the work of his ministry, informs the whole man of the plot devised, and appeals to the inner testimony of the soul's self-examination as the authority for these his sudden alarms and admonitions.

And Conscience appeals to the experience, too, as the inward witness that all is not well; he points to the evident decline of faith, the failing of hope, the coldness of love, and all the provocations whereby they "have sinned Immanuel out of the town." And the

experience thus awakened and appealed to testifies that an unlaw-
ful correspondence has been cultivated and encouraged between the
soul and Satan, to the downfall of faith, and the bondage of the once
freedom of the man of God.

When the Captains heard this.—After self-examination comes the
self-conviction of the soul, which is now made aware of the existence
and active energy of inward principles that have secretly devised
the ruin of its spiritual welfare. It is under these alarms, and by
means of these admonitions, that the Captains are now awakened
and aroused; for the once brave Captains of IMMANUEL have also
suffered sickness and decline, and thus the once pure gold has been
tarnished. Yes; Faith is in a low and sickly state; Hope is darkened
and beclouded; Charity has waxed cold; Patience has grown weary;
Innocence has been defiled; and the brave men of war, the strong
principles of the soul, have participated in the general decline, and
have suffered loss. But these great powers and principles of the
"new man" are now aroused by the tidings of self-examination, by
the alarms of conscience, and by the convictions of the soul; and,
accordingly, they address themselves to action.

These following particulars.—The arousing of the backslider to a
consciousness of his danger and peril puts the soul upon the taking
of due precaution to prevent the mischief, and to defeat the purpose
of hell. All the renewed principles are banded together for this—
"they agreed upon these following particulars:"—

1. Strict watch and ward of the gates, and of all that entered in
thereat. The "senses" are auxiliaries either to God or Satan. What
things the eyes see, and the ears hear, and the hands handle of,
have much to do with the tone of mind, and the degree of the soul's
health or sickness. Hence, the watchful vigilance of the soul in
securing the gates (the senses), and diligently examining the character of all the thoughts, and words, and scenes, and feelings that
would through them enter into the soul.

2. An equally strict search after those things that had already
been permitted to enter. Evil things lurk in the soul, cleave to the
memory, pollute the heart, and continue long as the hidden worm at
the root. And in a day of special watchfulness they will hide themselves all the more secretly, lest they be discovered and rooted out.

3. The total casting out of all that is Diabolonian in their nature.
Any principle of the man that has harbored any association of the
Diabolonian crew, shall be required openly to acknowledge the
wrong, and thus be made known as a traitor to the soul.

4. All the whole man—body, soul, and spirit—shall be humbled before God, in fasting, humiliation, and prayer. The flesh must suffer, that the spirit may be saved. The man shall deny himself his worldly business and his greed of gain, and thus strive to "keep under the body, and bring it into subjection."

5. And with humiliation shall be prayer, in which the soul will unveil its own sin, and tell it all into the ears of God, and make known all the secret depravity, the long-cherished evil, that has been brought to light by the self-examination of conscience.

6. And, besides all these, the spirit of self-examination shall be honored and magnified, as an expression of thankfulness for the past unveiling of the threatened danger, and as an encouragement to that godly principle in its future care for the interests of Mansoul. Self-examination is now henceforward invested with authority of search, as the inward eye and ear of the soul—"to pry, to see, and to hear."

The country where the Doubters were.—The subsequent efforts of self-examination are in the direction of the soul's doubts—the form in which the Diabolonian plot was to take effect. Hence the inward eye and ear are turned toward the land—the cloud-land—whence doubts come, and fears arise, and gloomy horrors take their source, when they gather round the soul, and rob it of its peace, and joy, and evidence, and happiness, and consolation.

The result of such an inward searching of the soul is to discover that the powers of hell are more or less near, and are coming on so fast as to demand instant action on the part of man, lest he be destroyed of the destroyer. Be it known unto all men that Satan *is* very near with his army of Doubt, and that it is man's spirit of Unbelief (old INCREDULITY) that is the chosen leader of the assault. All doubt and dark despair is caused by unbelief in man. If we truly believed the word, and promises of God, we might not indeed be without doubts, but we should be able to meet them boldly, and bravely to overcome them. We should, at least, meet them *in the light*, and this would be to rob them of their sharpest sting, and of their most deadly power.

A man once went out into the forest in the early twilight and under the morning mist. In the distance he thought he saw *a wild beast*, and he was afraid. By-and-by the fog began to clear, and, on nearer and better observation, he saw it was *a man*. Ere long the sun arose, and, behold, it was *his own brother!* In proportion to the darkness and the gloom were his suspicions; and in proportion to the rising and increase of the shining light, were those suspicions dispelled.

A diligent and impartial search.—It must be a "diligent" search. Such thorough searching of one's own soul is a personal matter; and no man can too curiously or inquisitively pry into his own spiritual concerns. Here, suspicion and examination never amount to an impertinence. Indeed, the more a man knows himself, and the eternal issue at stake, the more will he keep his eye upon himself. The more valuable the cargo, the more careful must be the custody. The nearer we approach the end, the more anxious we become, lest we should at last lose the prize; to be so near, and yet to lose it! Hence the words of the Psalmist—"I commune with mine own heart, and my spirit made diligent search," Psalm 77:6.

And this search of the soul must not only be "diligent," but "impartial" also. Sometimes we may search diligently, and yet, with a sinful partiality, spare the sins we find lurking within us. Some fondled treasure of the heart is spared, as "the best of the sheep and of the oxen" of Amalek were spared, only to draw down the heavier woe and the greater condemnation—"For rebellion is as the sin of witchcraft, and stubbornness is as iniquity and idolatry," 1 Samuel 15:23.

In this instance the search was both "diligent" and "impartial;" for the men of Mansoul searched thoroughly; and when they found the Diabolonian spoilers, disguised, in the houses of two of their ruling powers—the Mind and the Will—they spared them not, neither the servants nor the masters; the servants they utterly destroyed, and the masters they put to open humiliation and shame, albeit they were of the rulers of the land.

A very deep consumption.—There is something very striking and suggestive in Bunyan's description of the manner of the death of these two disguised Diabolonian principles—Covetousness (otherwise calling itself PRUDENT-THRIFTY) and Lasciviousness (whose assumed name was HARMLESS-MIRTH). Their death was not sudden, nor accomplished in a day; but they are first imprisoned, and, in their bondage, they pine away in deep consumption, and die.

This is the process through which most of our ingrained and inveterate sins must pass, ere the evil nature is utterly destroyed. These sins have been so fostered in us, have so rooted and grounded themselves in the evil heart, and so multiplied the fibers of their attachment to the soil, that it needs time, restraint, bondage, and the cutting off of every source of their life-supply, the digging deep to the lowermost and uttermost root, ere their vigor is impaired, their strength weakened, and their very being put out of remembrance. There is but little death of sin, because there is but little of the *dying* of sin within us. Ere this mortifying of the corrupt nature is fully accomplished, we must be able to say with the Apostle, "I die daily."

The manner of penance.—Bunyan does not employ the word "penance" in the sense in which it is used by the Church of Rome, in whose theology it is accounted as "a sacrament," and chiefly implies the works or penalties by which the members of that Church attempt a self-atonement for their sin. The word, as used in our allegory, is the old word for "penitence," which included the evidences of sorrow—"fruits worthy of repentance." This, indeed, is clearly stated in the context, in which Bunyan states the two main constituent elements, which are the sum and substance of true repentance, namely, confession of the past, and amendment for the future—"open confession of their faults, and a strict amendment of their lives."

Glad to shrink into corners.—Self-examination, when diligently and impartially conducted, is as a whip and a scourge to the evil nature. The lusts, and appetites, and tempers shrink from the lash, and hide in the darkness, away from the scrutiny of the searching light. Sins, like fugitives, are chased to dens and caves, and other hiding-places, where they live, if they can, and lurk and wait in secret ambush, biding the time of another opportunity. Therefore it is not enough to chase them to their corners; they must be thoroughly searched out and utterly slain. And Mansoul is still indebted to Mr. PRYWELL for this wondrous change. Let the soul take this counsel— "Know thyself;" and to attain this knowledge, let him add this also— "Examine thyself."

Diabolus had finished his army.—The self-examination and consequent vigilance of the soul do not, however, interrupt the preparations of Satan, or stay the expedition of the "terrible army" against Mansoul. The "plot" had been conceived and planned ere the town had awakened to a sense of its miserable state. Meanwhile, the soul has been aroused, and placed in a position of defense. The outer army is as before—enlisted, organized, and already on the march; but the Diabolonian allies from within have been sought out, and some of them slain, and the rest of them dispersed. But the great DIABOLUS knows not this. The spirit of INCREDULITY hovers not now, as at other times, over both encampments, moving to and fro, and bearing messages to his master. Nor does Mr. PROFANE go forth as the bearer of letters and communications from the house of Mr. MISCHIEF. The conspiracy has been disbanded; the conspirators have fled; and the natural allies of the Evil One cannot now render that aid from within which, in the day of their boasting, they had so confidently promised. So, now the chief reliance of DIABOLUS must be in the army he has raised for the assault—"the terrible army of Doubters!"

And this army has its "officers, colors, and scutcheons;" these being indicative of the elements that are banded and massed together by Satan against the soul, particularly when the soul is exposed to the assault of Doubt, and is under the bondage of Despair.

RAGE is there with his company of *election*-doubters, who, with *destructive* agonies of fear and desperation, rend and tear the soul. And FURY, over those who doubt the *vocation*, or effectual calling of God, and dwell in *darkness* that may even be felt. And DAMNATION, too, that cursed Captain of the lost, whose followers doubt the *grace* of God that bringeth salvation; and therefore is *no-life* found among them. And INSATIABLE is there, who doubts all *faith*, and pours his victims down the maw of the *devourer* that never says "Enough." And BRIMSTONE leads the van of those who stumble in the way, and doubt the *perseverance* of God's saints, and find their home in the everlasting *burnings*. And TORMENT, too, who even doubts the *resurrection* of the dead, and would consign the body to the *gnawing worm* of the grave for ever. And NO-EASE, with his ever *restless* standard, rallying the ill-fated souls who doubt the great *salvation*, And SEPULCHRE is there, leading forth the *glory* doubters, who would have men's glory "to see *corruption*," and leave nought but *dead men's bones* remaining. And last of all is PAST-HOPE, with *despair*, who knows not happiness nor joy, and leads the *felicity* doubters in his train.

Such were the Captains of the "terrible army;" and over these were set the superior captains—the princes of the pit, they that hold the chief seats in hell, they that were the sharers of their great lord's rebellion, and now are partakers of his condemnation; and over these again was INCREDULITY; and over him, as lord paramount, was the great DIABOLUS himself.

If any man is disposed to contemn this armament, or to despise this formidable expedition, he is unwise, and knows not his danger as he ought to know it. An army thus equipped, thus marshaled, and thus commanded, is an army that demands on our side all the strength and consistency that grace and goodness can bestow, that it be met and vanquished. Yea, and with all, we need to cry to the

Strong One for help; for only in Christ, the "Captain of our salvation," can we withstand in the evil day, and at last prevail.

Mansoul was now awake.—And it had need to be! Thanks to the awakening grace of God, that arouses the soul from the depth of its slumbers, to a sense of the greatness of its danger. Had Mansoul slumbered on, it had perished in its sleep, betrayed from within, and assaulted from without. But it was not so: grace and mercy hovered over its couch of slumber, and in time awaked the sleeper. The covenant, so far as man was concerned, was well nigh broken; but still the word continued true—"If God be for us, who can be against us?" Mysterious things are these "deep things of God!" that man should trifle to the very brink, and sin away his day of grace to almost the closing moment, and yet be saved! Surely, such salvation is of grace.

And now the soul is awakened, is alarmed, is vigilant, yea, is double watchful. It also resumes its former weapons—the slings and stones of the word and promises of God. The watchman stands upon the watch tower; the sentinel guards its gates; and self-examination searches out its secret places. Thus sovereign mercy hath appointed it, that his own purchased possession, the redeemed and ransomed soul, thus awakened out of its second sleep, should be prepared and ready to meet its spiritual foe, "as the host was going forth to the fight, and shouted for the battle!"

A furious assault.—This assault of hell was designed to carry all before it, and to make a final end. And yet it failed. It failed for lack of the expected action from within, that was to have co-operated with the assault from without. Inner treachery or weakness is more to be feared than the most formidable foe from without. Thus it was at the first, as stated at the outset of the Allegory, "that the walls could never be broken down nor hurt, by the most mighty adverse potentate, unless the townsmen gave consent thereto."

And on this occasion that "consent" was not given, but withheld. No gate opened to the foe, no voice from within counseled for surrender, no key was turned by a treacherous hand, no inner influence was found to second the outer violence. The soul stood, stern as a rock, "steadfast, immovable."

And the terrible doubts were accompanied by terrible fears. All that could affright or terrify was pressed into the service of DIABOLUS—the rising mounts of defiance, and their terrible names; the terrible standard, with its flaming flame, and its burning effigy; the beating of the terrible drum of the Doubters; and the nightly call to the soul for parley. Oh, how the soul of the doubting and despairing man fears the nightfall, and the darkness, and all the accompanying terrors intensified manifold in the night season!

But Mansoul resisted, fighting the good fight by day, and betaking itself to the Captains by night. In the time of peril, and in the hour of danger, our safety is in the company of the gifts and graces of the Spirit—under the shield of faith, under the helmet of hope, under the comforts of love, and in the sanctifying presence of patience and innocence. These abide in the stronghold of the man— the Castle, the heart. There, enshrined amid the holy things, surrounded by their great protection, the soul is in the chamber of peace, though the terrible army does still beleaguer it. "Thou shalt not be afraid for the terror by night; nor for the arrow that flieth by day; nor for the pestilence that walketh in darkness; nor for the destruction that wasteth at noonday," Psalm 91:5–6.

So Captain Sepulchre came up.—This is the last attempt of DIABOLUS to alarm the soul. Doubts are formidable enough in themselves; the rolling *rappel* of the drum of the Doubters is a yet greater aggravation of one's fears; but death and the grave are the most terrible of all—even the king of terrors. The doubting soul, that has lost its trust and confidence in Christ, and relaxed its hold of the promises of God, and forfeited the evidence of the witnessing Spirit—how that soul trembles at the thought of death, and is appalled at the terrors of the grave! It sees nought before it but corruption of the body, condemnation of the soul, the loss of all things here and hereafter. And, therefore, craftily superadded to other fears, is the dread of the grave, the cold sepulchre, the horrors of the comfortless tomb. And on the score of this universal penalty to sin, Satan claims Mansoul as his own peculiar property; and if their disobedience to his call should still continue, he threatens that he will "swallow them up as the grave."

Meanwhile, the eye of the soul's enlightenment is dimmed, and its power of faith weak, and its once hopes and joys terror-stricken; else would the soul be able to realize the better hope, and to give back this jubilant answer of faith to the taunting message of Captain SEPULCHRE—"O Death, where is thy sting? O Grave, where is thy victory?" Yes; when the doubts of the man of God cease, and his hopes, and joys, and evidence return, his faith rises superior to the fears of death, and through the grave and gate of death he sees "the blessed hope" of the resurrection-day—death of death, and hell's destruction. "Then shall be brought to pass the saying that is written, Death is swallowed up in victory," 1 Corinthians 15:54. And again, "That mortality might be swallowed up of life," 2 Corinthians 5:4. Captain SEPULCHRE may vaunt himself now, and, at the bidding of his master, demand the surrender of the soul to Satan; but the end cometh, as seen in the vision of the seer of Patmos—"And death and hell were cast into the lake of fire. This is the second death," Revelation 20:14.

CHAPTER XII

THE PRAYER OF MANSOUL

OUTLINE OF CHAPTER XII.—The Lord Secretary appealed to.—The Three Petitions.—The unfavorable Answer.—The Lord Mayor "picks comfort" out of it.—Mansoul waxes valiant in fight.—The Parley.—Diabolus fawns and flatters, but Mansoul is watchful.—The Lord Mayor answers.—The drum of the Doubters again.—The use of Mouth-Gate.—Further search for Diabolonians.—Executions.—Desperate Assault, and brave Resistance.—Loss on both sides.—The wounds of Mansoul healed.

The languishing town of Mansoul.—Not yet is the day of deliverance; the terrors and alarms continue, and though the soul fights manfully, yet doth it languish in the heat of the fray, and in the dust of the battle-field, and in the daily and nightly horrors of the terrible siege, environed by the army of Doubt, and by the legions of Despair. Nor is there any relief but in the holy confidence that the soul is enabled to repose on the promises of God, and on the aid of the all-powerful Immanuel.

> "In times like these we should
>   Be driven to despair,
> And in desponding mood
>   Give up all hope and prayer,
> Did God before our eyes
>   Not set forth his dear Son;
> His death and sacrifice,
>   And all that he has done!"

Applied to the Lord Secretary.—An illustration of the present state of the soul's spiritual health is conveyed in the message of the Spirit to the Church of Sardis—"I know thy works, that thou hast a name that thou livest, and art dead. Be watchful, and strengthen the things which remain, that are ready to die: for I have not found thy works perfect before God," Revelation 3:1–2. This would seem to be the phase of the soul's spiritual state at this crisis. The Spirit has withdrawn himself; IMMANUEL is gone; prayer is made, but is not answered; the Diabolonians revive, and wax wanton; plots are concocted, snares laid, and, under various disguises of name and dress, the principles of the evil nature are received into the service of the soul. Meanwhile, an army of terrible Doubters has gathered outside, and a conspiracy of the corrupt principles of the soul has been organized within, for the purpose of a treacherous co-operation with the assault of the invading army. This conspiracy has been discovered by the self-examination of the soul; the full tidings of the threatened danger have come to the ears of Mansoul; the whole man is set on watch and guard; and, so far, the soul's spirit of watchfulness and resistance has staved off the violence of the assault.

But this state of spiritual being is one that leaves the soul in a "languishing" condition. The man is here described as resisting the devil, striving against sin, and strongly antagonistic to the assault of doubt and desperation. And this is well and wisely done. The soul has been asleep, it must now awake; it has been remiss, it must now be active; it has suffered its Prince to depart, and must be made to feel the loss; it has seen the effort of DIABOLUS to regain his lost dominion, and it takes the alarm, and manfully resists.

It is at this crisis of affairs that the soul once more betakes itself to prayer. This time it is true prayer, and offered in the power of the Spirit. The soul seeks the Holy Spirit's aid. It is only through the influence of the Spirit that man can pray aright. The Spirit leads the soul to Christ, and Christ conducts the soul to God—"For through him (the Son) we both have access by one Spirit unto the Father," Ephesians 2:18. We have already been informed, in a previous stage of the Allegory, that the high office of the Spirit in the renewed soul is that of Chief Preacher and Adviser. He is *in* us, and he is *of* God—in communion with both, and conducting both into communion with each other. He is well and appropriately called the "Lord Chief Secretary," having knowledge of the secret mind and will of God—"For what man knoweth the things of a man, save the spirit of man which is in him? even so the things of God knoweth no man, but the Spirit of God," 1 Corinthians 2:11. Whatsoever we spiritually know of God and Christ is through the Holy Spirit—"All things that the Father hath are mine: therefore said I, that he (the Spirit) shall take of mine, and shall show it unto you," John 16:15.

But the Holy Spirit has been offended and grieved by the sin of Mansoul, and has withdrawn his countenance and counsel in the time of need. It is possible to "grieve," to "resist," to "despise," and even to "quench" the Spirit of God within us. It is only as he has a welcome, that he abides in our hearts. There is no more sensitive principle in man than the indwelling presence of the Spirit; none so easily offended; none so easily forfeited and lost.

Nevertheless, Mansoul now cleaves to the Spirit in prayer. And the praying soul, under a full appreciation of its wants and necessities, makes request for three things:—

1. For *audience*. Nothing is done until we have gained the *ear* of God. If our prayer rises not to the great audience-chamber, and enters not into the ears of the God of Hosts, that prayer is not heard, and therefore it is not answered.

2. For *advice*. Having gained the ear, we seek the *counsel* of the Spirit. He is the giver of that wisdom that cometh from above. And when could man need counsel and advice more than during a season of doubt, when conflicting feelings and perplexing thoughts leave the soul rent and torn, wounded and half dead?

3. For *help*. Like the interceding patriarch, the soul rises in its demands, but with fear and trembling—"Oh, let not the Lord be angry, and I will yet speak but this once!" It asks not only to be heard, not only to be advised, but also to be *helped*. It is in danger, and seeks relief; in doubt, and needs knowledge; in a state of loss, and asks for help. The help sought for is the Spirit's aid in prayer— to ask for the right thing, to ask in the right way, and to ask with such influence and authority as to ensure success. In all these respects the Spirit "helpeth our infirmities," and "maketh intercession for us," Romans 8:26.

All the answer he gave.—The Spirit returns an unsatisfactory answer to all these requests. God's Spirit "strives" with man, and thus tests the genuineness of his repentance. And now is the soul reminded of its past unfaithfulness, and left to itself to suffer the consequences of its sin.

This is the trial of faith and patience; the hard discipline of the soul; the rankling of the gaping wound that will not close; the irritation of the sore that will not heal. And when Christ is absent, and the Spirit grieved, and doubt, and sin, and Satan so terribly near, the soul is harassed and perplexed with a thousand fears.

Until he had picked comfort.—Yet is not the soul altogether comfortless. If we pray with the spirit, and with the understanding also, it is possible even yet to "pick comfort" out of the apparently adverse answer. It is the office of the understanding to see and to understand, to inquire, and scrutinize, and narrowly to pry into the messages of Heaven, and gather what comfort it can, to support the soul in this its weary waiting time.

The narrative of the Woman of Canaan is strikingly illustrative of this phase of the soul's anxiety (Matthew 15:21–28). We there read an illustration of faith under many aspects—the faith of a stranger, a Gentile woman; faith manifested in the face of great difficulties; faith without encouragement, yea, absolutely discouraged; faith rebuked, tested, tried, and yet, withal, triumphant; a faith that had learned to "pick comfort" out of answers apparently the most unfriendly and decisive of refusal.

First, the Gentile woman's faith was tried by *the silence* of Jesus— "He answered her not a word." This was not the silence that "gives consent," but rather that silence that depresses one, takes the heart out of one, corrodes the spirit, irritates the temper, provokes retaliation, and is to many a thousand times worse than a positive refusal. And yet this faithful woman "picked comfort" out of it, and continued to follow Jesus, with earnestness, strong crying, and resolute determination; and such is her importunity that the disciples feel themselves constrained to interfere, saying, "Send her away; for she crieth after us."

A second test of this woman's faith is found in *the refusal* of Jesus— "He answered and said, I am not sent but unto the lost sheep of the house of Israel;" not to you, a Gentile, but to the house of Israel. And even out of this positive refusal she still "picked comfort." Her faith gathers strength; it wrestles now. Jesus has broken silence, he has deigned to speak; and on that speech she now lays hold, doing and daring great things; and, notwithstanding this answer of Jesus, she clings to him, and "worshipped him, saying, Lord, help me!"— although I am a Gentile, and not of the house of Israel, yet (laying emphasis upon the word), "Lord, help *me!*" Her faith tells her that there is, there must be, power in Jesus to overleap the boundaries of nations, and to extend the benefits of his grace beyond the seed of Abraham, to all the sons and daughters of Adam.

And yet a third, and last, and this the sorest, test awaits her, in *the severe rebuke* of Jesus—"It is not meet to take the children's bread, and to cast it to dogs;"—to take the bread of these children (the Jews), and to cast it to such as you—*dogs* of the Gentiles! And yet, even out of this apparently unfriendly speech, she "picked comfort." She acknowledges the title, adopts the epithet, assumes the expression to be in all respects just and true, and thereupon proceeds to build the superstructure of her faith and hope, saying, "Truth, Lord: yet the dogs eat of the crumbs that fall from their masters' table!" She asked not, as a child, for the fullness of bread; but, as a dog, for the *crumbs*, the broken fragments that remain— only this, and it sufficeth, Lord! She "picks comfort," if only she can pick the crumbs!

And so, on this occasion, the understanding of the soul "picked comfort" out of the apparently unfriendly answer of the Spirit. It saw that the Spirit was purposed still to have dealings with the soul, and was minded to test it, and make it wait a little longer. The comfort thus gleaned was "the comfort of hope."

Began to take some courage.—After comfort is encouragement; and under these scanty consolations the soul fights on. Satan is near, the soul is troubled, doubt and despair are at the very gates, and the warfare still continues.

In this continued conflict there are two formidable elements—one on either side. There is the terrible "drum" of Diabolus, on the side of the Doubters; and there are the "slings" of the Prince, on the part of Mansoul. The one is all noise, turmoil, tumult, trouble, confusion worse confounded, the continual worry of the doubting soul. The other includes the comfort of the precepts, and the hope of the promises, of God's Word, which tell the soul that the covenant of Immanuel still continues; and these comforts refresh the soul.

Having all be-sugared his lips.—While the warfare continues the soul is strong. There is something bracing in the very exercise of the conflict; and something manly in learning the experiences of the battle-field. Therefore would Satan have the warfare cease. He loves to see the flag of truce—the white flag of the wearied and exhausted warrior, who would interrupt the strife in order to bury his dead, or to rest himself in the soft lap of pleasure or indulgence. Hence, Diabolus invites the warring soul to a parley; and seeks, with honeyed speech and sugared lips, to put the soul off its guard, and to deceive it as he had before deceived it.

And in this parley he speaks as though it were his love and friendship for the soul, his desire and zeal for its welfare, that prompted him thus to seek back and recover its lost allegiance to his throne. Sometimes cowering with a craven spirit, sometimes defying with a defiant air, he intermingles love and hate, promises and threatenings, showing the soul, though falsely, the conditions and consequences of the alternative that is now before it. He also reminds the soul of its present agitations and anxieties as compared with the ease and pleasure of its former service under sin, when no such deep feelings, or dark thoughts, or doubting fears, or sad surmisings, troubled it; when it lay in the lap of Satan, and was satisfied. He thus invites the soul once more beneath the power of his dominion; promises that these giant sins shall be servants, to serve, and not masters, to rule and govern; and, at last, magnifies the power of his fierce anger, the force of his mighty strength, the terribleness of his unquenchable wrath, in comparison of which Goliath and the giants of those days were as nothing, their strength but weakness, and all their might as a thing of no account.

Are there no parleys like this in our experience of our own back-slidings, and of Satan's efforts to re-possess our souls? Do none of the true Israel of God ever look back and sigh after the flesh-pots of Egypt? Are not our ears at times attentive to the comparisons of Satan's speech, when he contrasts the service of God with the former service to the flesh, and suggests the thought of a return to the dominion of carnal things? Satan does often thus address himself to the renewed soul, whispering thoughts of apostasy, faithlessness, and unbelief.

The Lord Mayor replied.—It is the part of the enlightened understanding to give the soul's answer back to Satan. When "the god of this world blinds the mind of them that believe not," the understanding is darkened, and it can cast back no bold words of positive refusal in reply to the devices of Satan. But now there is light beaming upon the eye of the soul. Accordingly, the understanding now replies; and it distinctly answers, No; boldly, and with a good conscience, it answers, No; under deep exercise of spirit, it answers, No; by the love it bears the Prince, it answers, No; in the full experience of the past, it answers, No; and in the interest of its future history, it answers, No. Aye, death rather than denial of the Prince!—the grave rather than surrender to Diabolus!

> "Well done! thy words are brave and bold;
>   At times they seem to me
> Like Luther's in the days of old,
>   Half battles for the free!"

And, indeed, this decisive action of the soul awakes the wrath of hell and Satan; and from the failure of his fawning speech he retires, breathing out threatening and slaughter against the bold principles of the anxious soul, which is now seeking to regain its lost evidence, and to recover the forfeited favor of Immanuel.

And thus disposed of his men.—DIABOLUS withdraws from the unsuccessful parley, for action on his side, which seems, however, to be
designed to alarm and terrify the soul with further terrors. He brings
up his captains and their hosts to the gates—so terribly near! These
are the doubts, and fears, and desperate thoughts of man gathering
round the soul, and assailing it in its outer frames and feelings.

For example, the feelings (Feel-gate) are made sensible of the
near approach of the terrible army; for Cruelty and Torment assail
the soul in that direction. Even Nose-gate, which seems hitherto to
have done but little service, for good or for evil, in this campaign, is
made sensitive to, and a partaker of, the horrors of the soul; for
Brimstone and Sepulchre send up their noisome exhalations,
making the terrors of the grave and of the pit to be almost realized
in actual experience. And the eye (Eye-gate) sees nought else but
darkness within the scope of its vision—the darkness of desolation,
the absence of all hope, the dismal prospect of dark despair. Such
are some of the expedients of Satan's wrath to subdue the soul to
the yoke of his dominion.

Mouth-gate for a sally-port.—Feel-gate, Nose-gate, Eye-gate—all
besieged; and yet Mouth-gate is not beleaguered! An effort, indeed,
was made to stop it with "dirt," that is, to fill the mouth with vile
words and blasphemies instead of with prayers and supplications,
but in vain. The power of prayer keeps Mouth-gate open, and keeps
it also pure and clean; and when Mouth-gate is open in prayer, it is
strongly fenced against the power of Satan. This gate is doubly
useful, both for prayer and for conflict.

Through Mouth-gate Mansoul prayed. The mouth is the highway
of prayer, from the heart of man to the throne of God. It is the
"sally-port" of the soul for supplication. Prayer is the preserver of
the soul, as the salt preserves the sea. Prayer is the pillar of the
soul, against which it leans, and supports its failing strength.
DIABOLUS may talk of Goliath, the proud Philistine, and disdain him,
as the Philistine disdained the stripling David; but, in the praying
soul, Satan has to deal with more than a Goliath; yea, the giant of
Gath stood not in half such strength! "O Lord, open thou our lips,
and our mouth shall show forth thy praise."

Through Mouth-gate Mansoul fought also. With the same armor
that Jesus used, when, in his conflict with Satan, he foiled the
tempter by the simple words—"It is written." And so, with the
sword of the Spirit, which is the Word of God, man still fights; and
from the "slings" of revelation he is enabled to dispatch the missiles

of the Lord—the precepts and promises of the Word. There is no more effectual way for slaying our doubts than by bringing forth against each doubt a *promise* of our covenant-keeping God.

Busy in preparing within.—No amount of prayer or conflict will suffice without inward watchfulness and the preparation of the heart. All the issues of good or ill success are from within; hence, the internal discipline of the soul continues. So long as DIABOLUS disposes his army from without, and has allies dwelling within, the soul must not abate one jot or tittle of its self-suspicion and self-examination. The thoughts, the desires, the appetites, the tempers, the passions, all need to be kept in subjection, under the yoke and beneath the heel of the conqueror. To withdraw the hand, or to relax the hold, is to encourage the lurking spirit of evil, and to give it fresh opportunity for revival in the soul.

In the exercise of self-discipline, the Will is most of all responsible. The Will of man keeps the entrance-gates of the soul; and it is by the leave and license of the Will that evil thoughts are permitted to tarry, and are entertained and encouraged, until by-and-by they have brought forth evil desires, and those again have fructified into evil deeds. How often does the soul thus wage an unequal warfare against the powers of evil, while the Will turns traitor, opens the gates, admits the foe, and harbors him in the region of volition and desire. The Understanding may know that it is wrong; the Conscience may loudly repudiate the act: but the Will loves to have it so. Then what can the soul do when the Will thus secretly inclines to the evil intent, and yields itself to the hands of the destroyer?

But if the will of man be in subjection to the will of God; if it bear the yoke and be under the influence of the Spirit of holiness, it will do valiantly in the interest of the soul; it will discover and destroy the remnant of the fleshly nature, and mortify and crucify the old man, with its affections and lusts. Such is the responsibility of the Will of man.

Jolly and Griggish.—One would think that Bunyan had borrowed, by anticipation, a part of the "slang" of our own age, when he indicates by these names the offspring of that Diabolonian principle, Lasciviousness, which disguised itself under the more deceptive name of Harmless-Mirth. The names here given to his two sons are, indeed, very suggestive, and point to those features of the worldly mind which include carnal pleasure, the mirth that hurts the soul, the laughter that makes one sad, and the joy of the world, that so soon turns to sorrow and bitterness. Worldly pleasure ofttimes relaxes the discipline of the soul; the bow unbent is subject to reaction; and that which seemed to be harmless, pleasurable, and mirthful, becomes the occasion of a deep decline of faith and holiness, and, at last, a grievous downfall of the soul. These principles must be put to the cross—crucified and slain; else, that which is the offspring of past sin may become the parent of future transgression.

This Christian act.—No disciplinary act of the soul can be without a result for good; or, as Bunyan notes in the margin of the original work—"Mortification of sin is a sign of hope of life." One such resolute act of the soul, in slaying any root of sin within it, is a grave discouragement to the army of Diabolus. The soul that can resist sin, and crucify the flesh, gives evidence of a power that will be able to destroy doubt, and to overcome despair. This resistance serves as a bracing discipline to the soul, which waxes yet more and more courageous, as its hand cleaveth to the sword of successful conflict.

Gripe and Rake-All.—These, again, are the offspring of the disguised Diabolonian nature—the well-named children of Prudent-Thrifty, more truly called by the name of Covetousness. See how vain it is to change the *name* of any evil principle: its nature remains the same, and familiarity with it breeds bitter fruit. In this case, the soul harboring the lust of gain, becomes grasping and greedy, and, to all intents and purposes, the slave of covetousness. This remnant or outgrowth of the old man must also be destroyed. The mind must act with vigor, and deal honestly with itself; it must cast mere *names* to the winds, and regard the true *nature* of things. Thus only can the evil heart be thoroughly searched out and examined, and sin exterminated, root and branch.

Furious madness and rage.—Satan's wrath is better to the soul than Satan's favor. When he flatters and fawns, there is lurking danger; but when he fights, and is wroth, and is mad, the soul may take encouragement as well as warning.

Resistance is the duty and the safety of the Christian soldier; for, though it may tend to provoke the enmity of hell, and to augment the rage of Satan, and the brunt of the battle may wax hotter and hotter, and so continue for many days of conflict; yet is this discipline healthful to the soul; its doubts decline, and its hopes increase. Resist, and doubt retires; sheathe the sword, and you are instantly overwhelmed by doubt. The soul is now resisting the devil, and, with various successes, the fight goes bravely on, and Mansoul fights the good fight of faith.

A surgeon was scarce in Mansoul.—Now that Immanuel has departed it may be asked,—"Is there no balm in Gilead? is there no physician there?" Jeremiah 8:22. The soul has no healing power of itself; it can hurt, but it cannot heal. Christ being absent, the physician of the soul is absent, and the man lies bleeding in his wounds, until help arrives, and is administered by some dispensation of the grace of God.

The leaves of a tree.—The allusion here is to "the tree of life," whose leaves were "for the healing of the nations," Revelation 22:2. We are also reminded here of the sequel to CHRISTIAN's great encounter with APOLLYON, as narrated in the PILGRIM'S PROGRESS:—"Then there came to him a hand, with some of the leaves of the 'tree of life,' the which CHRISTIAN took, and applied to the wounds that he had received in the battle, and was healed immediately." It is the same phase of the soul in both allegories: the conflict, the close conflict of the soul with Satan, provoked by man's shortcoming and remissness, and causing much damage to the soul. Even though victory may at the last crown the conflict, yet it is not a bloodless victory, nor altogether without loss. The soul is wounded in the fray, and it may be yet many days ere even the leaves of the tree of life restore the soul, and heal its "wounds, and bruises, and putrefying sores."

Yet is there a healing balm for the sin-sick soul, and a medicine for every wound that is received in the good fight of faith, and in the service of the King. If we fight under the banner of Christ as good soldiers of the cross, and are wounded, He whose servants we are will not suffer us to die, but will visit us with the joy of his salvation, and with the saving health of his right hand.

> "Rejoice, oh, heaven! be glad and sing;
>   Send from the tree of life
> The healing balm of Gilead's King,
>   To heal the wounds of strife."

These were wounded.—There is here given a detailed description of the character and extent of the loss incurred by the soul in its conflict with doubt and desperation. Such seasons of sore conflict with the fears and fancies, the doubts and uncertainties, of the backsliding soul, are calculated to do serious hurt and injury to the principles of the once man of God.

The Reason is affected, being unsettled by the opposition of rising doubts, which argue against the man's former faith, and strive to overturn the ground and evidence upon which that faith has been established. The Understanding suffers violence;—the eye of the understanding is dimmed and darkened, so that it sees not, nor perceives, as clearly as before. The Mind, too, suffers loss, and is unable spiritually to digest the food it has received. And even the Conscience is sore wounded, in the clash of conflicting doubts, and fears, and apprehensions. These casualties, however, which had befallen the principles of the soul were not mortal; but, at the same time, many of "the inferior sort," which Bunyan interprets to mean "hopeful thoughts," were slain. Doubt and despair cause many a holy thought, many a hopeful promise, and many a joyful experience to die within us. Like as in the assault upon LITTLE-FAITH, he retained, indeed, the "jewels" of the kingdom, but he lost his "spending money"—that is, his joy, and hope, and consolation. Yet, for the healing of all these sores and sorrows of the wounded soul, the "leaves of the tree of life" sufficed.

Were wounded and slain.—There is no healing medicine to restore the wounded of the army of DIABOLUS; they that are wounded there *die* of their wounds. "Wounded and slain," except, indeed, sin revives them. Doubt and unbelief must, therefore, be vigorously dealt with, without mercy, and with an unsparing hand. In the utter death of these consists the soul's life, and health, and well-being.

Victory turned to Mansoul.—The tide of battle turns in favor of the militant soul, while thus consistently waging its holy warfare against the power of indwelling sin, and the opposing wrath of Satan. The same Word of God that supplied the Key of Promise to the Pilgrims in Doubting Castle, and opened up a way of escape, now supplies the "slings" by which the army of Doubt is driven back, and the balance of victory inclines to MANSOUL. God's Word is ever as a light to them that are in darkness; a comfort to them that are in doubt; a prop and stay to them that are weak; a source of hope and joy to them that are cast down; the best weapon of defense of the soul's comfort and peace; and the surest weapon of offence against the onset of the powers of darkness and the deep. The mourning soul is now turned to gladness, and enjoys its seasons of rest, repose, and thankfulness.

> "For Thee, O God, we fight;
>   May we be strong in Thee;
> Receiving of thy strength and might
>   For final victory!
> Rejoice, I say, rejoice,
>   On this glad, holy day;
> And lift to heaven a mighty voice,
>   And shout of Victory!"

Mr. Anything.—When the soul, fighting the good fight, gains the upper hand, the hidden things of darkness are more and more brought to light, and put to open shame. The spirit of indifference, for example, is one of the first to be thus dealt with, as involving serious danger to the soul. Religion is a definite, decisive thing, and cannot consist with a careless, reckless, indifferent tone of mind. It generally happens that *any* religion means *no* religion. The soul that has been much and deeply exercised in doubt, and has resisted and fought against it, and overcome it, will all the more highly prize the truth when it has ascertained it, and will scarcely be disposed to entertain that spirit of indolent indifference that sees and makes no distinction between truth and error. Hence, with the disciplined soul, Mr. ANYTHING finds no place.

And so, also, the spirit of communication between the soul and Satan is now sought and discovered in the character of LOOSE-FOOT. The evil thoughts are swift of foot to find their master, and to communicate to him the evil intentions and desires of the carnal mind. It is this constant and speedy interchange of thought that so defiles the spirit of man with the counsels of Satan. This mysterious messenger of the soul must, therefore, be bound in chains, and by-and-by led forth to die. These two Diabolonian principles are under the jurisdiction of the will; and in proportion as the will of man is in accordance with the will of God, it will subdue the rising spirit of indifference, and bind in chains the evil thoughts and desires that would go out seeking after Satan.

All his good documents alive.—Conscience has much to do with the maintenance of the soul's health, by faithfully fulfilling its office as the preacher and adviser of MANSOUL. The carnal memory would forget the things of God, so the spiritual memory must keep them in remembrance. And as these things are day by day re-impressed and deepened, and kept alive in the tablet of the heart, man will be a law unto himself, having the law written upon his heart, and the Word of God as a *living* testimony abiding in the soul. The conscience, in its relationship to man, may adopt the words of the Apostle:—"Yea, I think it meet, as long as I am in this tabernacle, to stir you up by putting you in remembrance," 2 Peter 1:13.

So far, all seems well: the soul is prayerful, watchful, diligent, valiant, hopeful. Meanwhile, the warfare is not yet ended, and MANSOUL must continue to fight for the mastery.

CHAPTER XIII

A MIDNIGHT SORTIE

OUTLINE OF CHAPTER XIII.—Presumption.—An Unseasonable Expedition.—Credence, Experience, and Good-Hope Wounded.—Rout and Retreat of Mansoul.—Diabolus Encouraged.—Demands Surrender.—The Lord Mayor and Willbewill resist.—Assault by night on Feel-Gate.—The Diabolonian Watchword.—The Gate yields, and is broken open.—Diabolus Enters.—The Townsmen retreat to the Castle.—The Town overspread by the Doubters.—Desolate State of Mansoul.—The Castle holds out, and is besieged.—Mr. Godly-Fear the Keeper of the Castle.—No Surrender!

The folly of Mansoul.—The scene now changes; clouds again overcast the sky; darkness lowers; and the wisdom of Mansoul, the wisdom the soul has been learning in the school of hard experience, is about to be turned into foolishness—"the folly of Mansoul." And at this point the Allegory again turns to admonitions, and bids the soul—"Beware!" The past successes of the warfare have made the soul to wax presumptuous, to confide overmuch in its own strength, and to undervalue the real force of the enemy. It is possible for the soul to be over-confident of its own resources, and to become impetuous and rash in the spiritual conflict. This is a dangerous downfall. The soul cannot afford to trifle. The interests at stake are too vital and important to be trifled with. Satan is a wily general, and he will outwit us if he can; and at times he contrives to make the very successes of the soul to issue in sad reverses, by encouraging the over-weaning spirit of self-confidence. How ofttimes does the soul lay down its arms after a successful engagement with the spiritual foe, but long ere the full campaign is completed, and the warfare accomplished! or, how often, as in this case, does the soul venture forth presumptuously, and at inopportune seasons, for an unprovoked renewal of the fight! "Let not him that girdeth on his harness boast himself as he that putteth it off," 1 Kings 20:11.

To provoke temptation, to dare unbidden dangers, forms no part of a man's duty. In this sense the words of the wise man spiritually apply—"To everything there is a season, and a time to every purpose under the heaven: a time of war, and a time of peace," Ecclesiastes 3:1, 8. Seeing that the soul of man is naturally prone to evil, and circumstances ever exist around him to incline and draw his heart thither, it behoves the soul to be wary and cautious, and to dare no unnecessary danger, and provoke no needless conflict. The soul is here described as provoking the spiritual encounter, at a time most favorable to the foe, and most adverse to its own interests. The darkness intensifies the danger; alarms and affrights the soul; renders it difficult to distinguish between friend and foe; and generally proves disastrous to that side which is less accustomed to fight in the dark. Then the thoughts, both good and evil, mingle promiscuously in the dark encounter; and the soul knows not how to distinguish between its hopes and its fears, between its joys and its despondings.

The Prince's captains fought.—The choicest of the captains, too, are embroiled in this unseasonable strife—CREDENCE, GOOD-HOPE, and EXPERIENCE. And these brave ones fought nobly and well, as faith, and hope, and Christian experience might be expected to do. They were the captains best adapted for a dark encounter: for Faith has a far-seeing eye, and a trusty hand, and it never walks by mere sense or sight; and Hope is the proper antagonist of doubt, whether by night or day; and Experience has already fought his way through dark battle-fields, and purchased to himself a good degree by all that he has learned, and taught, and done.

Captain Credence stumbled and fell.—The reverse that now befalls the soul is owing to the weakness and failing of faith; and this failing of the strength of faith is not during the hand-to-hand encounter, but in the subsequent "pursuit." This is, no doubt, intended to show what is the office and proper business of faith—to fight face to face against the spiritual enemy, but not to *pursue* a retreating foe. Faith is for the defense of the soul, and it is strong so long as it abides in or near to the heart. When it departs far away, it leaves the soul weak, and makes itself weak.

But faith is *wounded* now; and, although it is lifted up, it cannot stand. And this leads to further casualties and disasters. Faith, when strong and of a good courage, is the crowning grace of Mansoul; but faith, when wounded and weak, is indeed the "beginning of sorrows" to the man of God. When faith is wounded, then our hope is panic-stricken, and experience faints within us; all is disorder and derangement.

And this is Satan's opportunity. The hot pursuit abates its force; the soul has outrun its strength; and the "terrible army" is no longer pressed by the pursuers. That immediate danger over, Satan once more takes courage; and first "makes a stand," to consider what he had best to do; then "faces about," resolved to renew the fight; and so "comes up"—and, this time, on a wounded, weak, and fallen foe.

Safe into the hold again.—It had been well they had not left it. Presumption was the beginning of Babel, and confusion was the end of it. And so, in this phase of the soul's history, presumption led it forth on its unbidden errand, and it is driven back in swift retreat, with bleeding wounds, and sore confusion; its chiefest and its strongest principles—its faith, and hope, and tried experience—all placed *hors de combat** by that terrible night's untimely work. And well is it that, from the peril without, there is a retreat within; that the heart is still open to receive the returning gifts of God, and is straight closed again, to withstand the now renewed assault of Satan!

Diabolus was so flushed.—Flushed with victory, mad with rage, and hopeful of the issue, Satan assumes the offensive, so soon as faith fails or is made weak. And now he "promises himself" many things, while the soul sees no promise of any good; for the eye of faith, and the strength of hope, and the power of experience are faint and low. Satan approaches the soul with "boldness" now, and makes urgent "demands" upon its fidelity. When Mansoul is weak, then is DIABOLUS strong. When the master is bold, the servants partake of his confidence; and so the Diabolonians within the soul resume somewhat of their former courage. From within and from without the soul is threatened with imminent danger.

The Lord Mayor replied.—Though faith is feeble and faint, yet is Mansoul watchful. The Understanding is not now darkened as before; nor has "the god of this world" blinded its spiritual eye-sight. It was the office of the Understanding to "read in the revelation of mysteries," and thus to be the adviser of the soul. Already we have found how he had "picked comfort" out of the mysterious message of the Lord Chief Secretary (the Holy Spirit); and now we find him again reading the mysteries of God, and taking courage and comfort from the fact that the Prince, though absent, is yet *alive;* and while life remains in the covenant-keeping God, Mansoul shall belong to none else. Yes, this is a comforting and encouraging truth—"He ever liveth."

Willbewill stood up.—The Will of man, always so able an ally, for

---

*Hors de combat—out of combat; disabled from fighting.

good or evil, now exercises his all-important office in strong resistance to the demands and assaults of Diabolus. His charge is over
the "walls" and the "gates," and involves a double watchfulness—(1)
that the assailing force be not permitted to enter from without; and
(2) that the lurking Diabolonians shall not co-operate with them
from within.

The "senses" must now be closely guarded, and the "flesh" also
kept in subjection; for it is through these that evil thoughts enter
into the mind, and evil deeds go forth. It is in the power of the Will
to encourage or else to discourage the rebels; to admit and entertain
them, or to resist and slay them. On this occasion the Will is resolute for good, and bids them to their dens again. Both by words and
deeds does Willbewill prove himself a valiant man.

Hurricaning in Mansoul.—This is a significant mode of expressing
the wild and wanton ways of sin, when it feels itself in any measure
at liberty in the heart of man. Like the pent-up winds, released
from their prison-house, the evil principles of the corrupt nature
run riot, and play havoc in the soul. The breathing of a breath
becomes a breeze, and this ere long becomes a storm, and this,
waxing more presumptuous, buffets the soul with tempest-wrath, so
that it reaps the whirlwind.

All their force against Feel-gate.—With what violence and rage is this
assault conducted! The very cry of the assailants, the watchword of the
Doubters, would be sufficient to terrify the stoutest. But when the poor
doubting soul, that has trifled with sin, and put from it its evidence,
and lost the vigor of its faith and hope, and forfeited the comforts of its
past experience—when such a soul is surrounded by doubts and fears,
and hears the whispered word, "Hell-fire;" and these whispers wax
loud, and louder, and yet louder still, and are as the cry of terror, and
as the shriek of the troubled spirit, that cannot be at peace, and will
not rest; and night and day the sound is heard, and ceases not, while
the ears are made to tingle with the hellish cry, and with the terrible
drum of the Doubters—how can that soul be happy? or with what
resistance can it fight against such desperate odds?

The army of doubt always assails the *feelings;* and this is the
weak point of too many believers, especially when their faith is
wounded, their experience low, and their hope laid prostrate. When
faith is full, and strong, and sure, it triumphs over mere feeling, and
subordinates all the rising doubts and fears to its dominion and
command. The feelings demand palpable evidences—but faith is
satisfied with the promise of Jesus. The unbelieving Jews sought to

see "signs and wonders;" but the nobleman, exercising implicit faith, "believed *the word* that Jesus had spoken unto him, and he went his way," John 4:48–50.

These gates were but weak.—As faith is strong or weak, so are the feelings weak or strong; and at this crisis faith is very weak, and therefore are the gates assailable, and likely to yield to even a gentle pressure. It is the work of the night-time, too, when the doubting soul is more than ever susceptible of alarms. Satan, moreover, sets the torments and terrors of his terrible army as the watchful sentinels of the gate of feeling. Faith and the other holy principles of the soul make resistance, but very feebly, for they are wounded, and faint, and weary. And now, notwithstanding the covenant of grace, and the manifold gifts of the Spirit, and the past experience of the man of God, Satan again enters the outer gate of Mansoul. The flesh is subject to his dominion; the senses and feelings are held in his iron grasp; the thoughts, and hopes, and fears are dealt with according to his will; and only *the heart* is left, and he now seeks that, to take, subdue, and finally possess it.

Betook themselves to the Castle.—This is the one, only, and last re- treat of the soul. This lost, all is lost; this surrendered, the covenant is broken; this retained, all may yet be restored as at the first. "Out of the heart are the issues of life!" Thither the captains and the host retired; all the holy principles, and thoughts, and desires, and affections, and hopes of the soul congregated there, as in the inner shrine of the Holy One.

Ah, poor Mansoul!—The description of the state of Mansoul at this critical juncture enables Bunyan to draw a picture of the condition of a soul laboring under the thraldom* of Satan's tyranny. Holy thoughts conceived in the soul are scarce brought to the birth when their life is quenched within them; yea, "those that were yet un- born"—holy thoughts not yet brought forth, prematurely perish. Unholy violence is done to the more gentle, weak, and sensitive feelings and compassions of the soul. Fresh acts of cruelty and wrong are perpetrated upon the Conscience, which becomes more and more restless and uneasy; and upon the Understanding, which is somewhat blinded and darkened by the ravaging horde; and particularly upon the Will, because of the mighty power he wields in Mansoul; or as the margin would interpret it—"Satan has a particu- lar spite against a sanctified will."

---

*Thraldom—slavery or bondage.

They were not entertained.—The success of the Doubters, after all, is but an uneasy triumph; for they are neither welcomed nor entertained. Doubt is not a welcome visitant to the soul; it comes with an armed force, and takes violent possession, and is regarded by the soul much in the same way as a foreign army of occupation would be by a subjugated province—its only purpose being to vex, and harass, and disturb the peace; to trample down the fields and vineyards, and to devour the growing harvests. The Will of man does not co-operate from within; man does not willfully or willingly offend; he is under tyranny and oppression, and just now he cannot get forth to liberty and freedom.

But, above all, the Diabolonian army is refused admittance to the Castle; and this is the reason the soul is not utterly consumed. The heart is not only the citadel for safety and defense, but is also the stronghold of resistance and offence against the invading foe. From the heart the "slings" are played—that is, the promises go forth for the slaying of doubt, and for the comfort of the soul. And GODLY-FEAR is there, safe, and sound, and whole; an unwounded warrior the keeper of the Castle-gates. While this godly principle abides, and the heart holds out and yields not, Mansoul is safe from final woe, and Satan's victory is incomplete. The fear of God in the heart is a brave keeper of the soul.

About two years and a half.—We have already said that all this description of the terrible army of the Doubters is a reproduction of Bunyan's own spiritual biography and experience, as more fully stated in his "Grace Abounding;" especially as to the duration of certain periods of the soul's doubt and desperation, where he says, "Now was I as one bound; I felt myself shut up unto the judgment to come; nothing now *for two years together* would abide with me, but damnation, and an expectation of damnation" (sec. 142).

Well may Bunyan describe the agonies of the doubting soul, and thus in the light and shadow of his own experience say, "This was now the state of the town of Mansoul." Oh, that some Key of Promise may be found, to open the iron lock of this captivity; some ray of hope, to cheer the captive; some star of expectation, to shed a light upon the future path of Mansoul!

> "Oh, I do pray thee, Lord, to lead thy child—
>   Safe from this doubt, this anguish, and this pain;
> Whatever way thou pleasest through the wild,
>   So it but take me to thy home again!"

CHAPTER XIV

"BEHOLD, HE PRAYETH!"

OUTLINE OF CHAPTER XIV.—Renewed Prayer of Mansoul.—Advice of Godly-Fear.—Petition to the Prince.—Accredited and promoted by the Lord Chief Secretary (the Holy Spirit).—The Spirit "maketh intercession."—Captain Credence the Bearer of the Petition.—The Prayer.—Diabolus chides the Town.—Diabolus harangues the Diabolonians.—Renewed Demands of Diabolus.—Answer of Godly-Fear and the Lord Mayor.—Return of Credence.—Reports to the Town.—The Prince's gracious Answer.—The five Notes of the Prince.—Communion with the Spirit.—Credence promoted to the chief place.—Mansoul waxeth stronger and stronger.

This sad and lamentable condition.—The allegory just now describes the condition of the soul as being dark and gloomy enough: doubt has entered, and overspread the whole man, and has possessed all, except the heart. Satan assails this stronghold, but without success. Neither the Understanding, nor the Will, nor the Conscience feel disposed to yield. The influence of Godly-Fear, too, abides in the heart, so that it is not surrendered to the demands of Satan. We may, therefore, still have hope that all shall yet be well.

To draw up another petition.—Prayer has been tried, but in vain. No answer of peace has been vouchsafed. The soul had sought the Holy Spirit's help and guidance, but an indefinite reply was all that was granted in return. It was as though the prophet's description of the dealing of the Lord with his people were now true respecting his dealing with Mansoul—"Therefore it is come to pass, that as he cried, and they would not hear; so they cried, and I would not hear, saith the Lord of hosts," Zechariah 7:13.

It was only by reason of the far-seeing eye of the enlightened understanding that any, even a small measure of hope and comfort, could be entertained; and this was rather "picked out"—that is, inferred or elicited from the terms of the reply—than actually expressed in the Holy Spirit's answer.

The Lord Secretary's hand.—To pray "with the spirit, and with the

understanding also," is to pray faithfully and successfully. The
spirit of man must be in communion with the Spirit of God. The
counsel of Mr. GODLY-FEAR well describes the true nature and character of prayer. It must be offered and presented under the influence and guidance of the Holy Ghost. To this end, it must be the
work of the Spirit—his thoughts, his words, his suggestions giving
expression to our wants. And this prayer is known and recognized
in heaven; it has come from the Spirit of God; and through the
intercession of the Son of God, it is accepted before him. The Spirit
teaches us how to pray; instructs us as to our real wants, and thus
teaches us what to pray for; breathes life into the prayer, so that,
like a chain of communication, alive in every link, it shall convey
our message to the ears of God, and bring back the return-message
to our souls.

I will draw up a petition.—The Spirit undertakes the cause of man;
and what a marvelous description is here given of the nature and
character of true prayer! It begins and ends with the influence and
help of the Spirit; man, in the meantime, doing his part. The prayer
of faith is both human and Divine—a blending of the Divine suggestion and human effort. It must be characterized by the expression of
man's wants; and it must be accredited and strengthened by the
influence of the Spirit, and by the intercession of the Son; or, as
Bunyan well expresses the idea—"The hand and pen shall be mine,
but the ink and paper must be yours."

Captain Credence should carry it.—Now that the Spirit of God moves
the soul to prayer, the supplication thus instituted and promoted is
borne by the principle of *faith* to the audience of the Prince. There is
no out-going of the soul that can bear petitions so near to the ear
and heart of God as this principle of believing faith. It is the motive
power that speeds the arrow most directly and most surely to the
mark. The prayer of faith is a saving prayer, James 5:15. And
though the faith of Mansoul is wounded, and not yet fully restored,
yet is it willing to undertake this mission on behalf of the highest
and best interests of man.

The contents of the petition.—The petition is characterized by one
element throughout—confession of sin. The soul tells in the ear of
the Prince the full tale of its own misery and corruption—how all is
sin and backsliding from God; how this has brought about the
terrible woe and dreary desolation of all former peace and blessedness; how the Doubters and Diabolonians have possessed the soul;
how the indwelling Spirit has been grieved, and the once welcome

gifts and graces of the Spirit (the Captains) have been neglected, exposed to danger, wounded, and brought down to a low and sickly state; how IMMANUEL has departed and gone, and no prayer has brought back any answer of peace or promise. Then there is a plea for pity, a cry for mercy, and an appeal for help. And Faith speeds this confession and supplication to the throne and mercy-seat of Jesus.

Carried it out at Mouth-gate.—The promptings of the heart are ex-pressed by the utterances of the mouth, by the words of the lips. The *matter* of prayer consists of the thoughts and motives of the heart, influenced by the Spirit of God; but the *manner* of prayer includes the form and way in which these thoughts find expression. God can see the heart; his ear can hear the eloquence of thought as well as the eloquence of language. But still, God desires that men should pray in words, and designs that the mouth should thus second the feelings of the heart. Besides, it is good for man that he should utter definite words in prayer. Prayer that is merely mental may, possibly, become unreal, visionary, and purely contemplative. Words may not, indeed, be necessary to command the attention of God, but they are certainly useful to man, as being the expression of his thoughts and wants; they tend to keep him to the point of his prayer; and serve as way-marks, that he lose not himself in the multitude of his thoughts.

Then said Diabolus.—Prayer provokes the wrath of Satan, and caus-es him instantly to appeal to the Diabolonian principles that have beset the soul. He knows the strength of indwelling sin, and how much it is to be relied upon. He therefore suffers not the carnal nature to slumber, but alarms it, and awakes it, and provokes it to jealousy against the Spirit that is now thus effectually striving with man; and to the awakened evil nature he gives full liberty and license for every evil work. All good conceptions and holy thoughts are given over to destruction. All that is new and all that is old, of the better nature in man, is doomed to utter ruin. Shall Satan's wrath prevail? Nay, "for the elect's sake those days shall be shortened!"

Went up to the castle gates.—Satan, not content with afflicting the soul, proceeds to make a bold demand upon its defenders, that they resign their sacred trust, and surrender the heart to his dominion. But the fear of God, still abiding in man, will not permit this; yea, it even stoutly resists the demand. And in this answer of GODLY-FEAR we observe fear and faith combined, duty and confidence conjoined. The demand is summarily rejected, and confidence expressed that God will yet establish the soul, and visit it with perfect peace, 1 Peter 5:10.

Mr. Fooling.—Amid the earnest strivings of the soul, and its better thoughts and resolutions, there will yet at times intervene some secret whisper of the evil nature—some rebellious thought that would counsel foolishness, some remnant of the old nature that would still make itself heard, some representative of the old Adam rising up in the soul to counteract its better feelings, and to weaken or modify its good intentions. Such is this principle, Mr. FOOLING.

It is ever the design of Satan to withdraw the strong principles from the soul, if he possibly can. Thus, at the first, he caused Captain RESISTANCE to be slain, knowing that once this warring principle were quenched, the soul would soon fall an easy prey into his hands. And now he desires that CREDENCE should be delivered up, knowing very well that "without faith it is impossible to please God," and that it is the faith of Mansoul that most of all binds it to IMMANUEL. Captain CREDENCE has proved already how essential is his presence in the soul. He is the chief warrior in the fight; it is he that leadeth the hosts to the battle; it is he that speeds the petitions of the soul to heaven; he can wrestle with the principalities and powers of hell, in the battle of the warrior; and he can wrestle with God in prayer, in the interest of the soul. It is, indeed, only the intense folly of the soul that could advise the surrender of a principle so brave and so essential as this. And it is the duty of Godly-Fear in man to resist this folly, showing that for the soul to forfeit its faith is to forfeit everything. No man can afford to part with the faith that is in him.

A season of grace.—There are days of gloom and sadness, days of doubt and darkness, and there are also days of sunshine, and seasons of grace, accorded to the soul. A "season of grace" is a time of joy and fullness of faith, when, itself laden with the burden of the Lord, it communicates the tidings to the soul, and fills it "with all joy and peace in believing." Faith never bears a message to its Lord in vain; it never returns empty-handed to the soul that hath sent it forth as the bearer of its petitions. Large is the promise that is made to the prayer of faith—"And all things whatsoever ye shall ask in prayer, believing, ye shall receive," Matthew 21:22.

Something in general.—Faith bears a general answer to the soul—an all-diffusing evidence of peace, overspreading the soul with joy and gladness. There is a renewal of confidence and assurance, by reason of this general message of faith, that "all would be well at last."

Something in special.—There are also special and particular answers conveyed to the soul by Faith; and these are the more definite and appreciable comforts of the man of God. A word in season, a special word, is addressed to each member and to each principle of the spiritual man; so that each and all are strengthened. The ruling powers of Mansoul had, so far, done their duty, and had well fulfilled their parts. They have been tried and tested, they have boldly and successfully resisted, and with a jealous care they have held the heart for Christ; and now they have the reward of his approbation. "God is not unrighteous, that he will forget your works, and labor that proceedeth of love."

These special communications to the soul are here described as being made known in the form of "notes" or letters, addressed to the renewed principles respectively.

"The first Note" is addressed to the Understanding. He was, as it were, the eye of the soul. To his quick perception the soul is indebted for many things. It was his ripened judgment, and his deep study of "the revelation of mysteries" (which was also part of his office), that enabled him to "pick comfort" out of the apparently adverse reply of the Lord Chief Secretary, and thus, in the midst of gloom and darkness, his far-seeing eye could discern the rising of the light; and now that the light had arisen, he is one of the first to see it, and to rejoice in its consolation.

"The second Note" is addressed to the Will. This power had received command over the flesh and the senses—the external avenues by which the Evil One assails the soul. It was for the Will to subdue the body, and to keep it in subjection. We have read of the valiant deeds of this strong power of the new man—how it became the scourge of the lurking Diabolonians; how it chased them from the open and public gaze into their hiding-places, and pursued them even thither, and dragged them to the cross for execution; and how it avenged the great Master's cause, and tended to sanctify the wills and affections of the soul. Well may we offer up that beautiful prayer—

"Renew my *will* from day to day,
Blend it with thine, and take away
All that now makes it hard to say,
    'Thy will be done!'"

"The third Note" is for the Conscience of the renewed man. As "the subordinate preacher," he had well fulfilled his part, in warning, and admonishing, and alarming, and arousing, and teaching, and instructing the soul. And this office has been no sinecure in Mansoul, even during the period of its renewed state. Oft has it been needful to awake the soul from unbidden, untimely, and unhallowed sleep, from carnal security and unconcern; oft has the soul been called to humiliation, and fasting, and prayer, for its forgetfulness of God, and its departure from his ways; oft has the Word been drawn forth as the "sword of the Spirit," sharp and powerful, and by its threatenings and admonitions has brought the soul to penitence and prayer: all this has been effected by the ministry of Conscience, working in man, "reproving, rebuking, exhorting."

"The fourth Note" is addressed to the principle of Godly-Fear in the soul. Honor is conferred by IMMANUEL upon this element of the spiritual nature. Where the fear of God is found, Satan has not attained full mastery; and this is the bond that holds the soul to God. It was this principle that exposed the true character of the spirit of Carnal-Security, showing how it throws man off his guard, and leaves him an easy prey to the teeth of the destroyer. This was also the chosen keeper of the gates of the heart, and by reason of its safe custody under his hands, the heart had held out thus long against the terrible army of Satan. Godly-fear, likewise, prompts man to prayer, and urges the soul to the duty of dependence upon its helper, its Savior, its God. Therefore, by reason of its past service, this faithful servant is promised his reward.

"The fifth Note" was written "to the whole town of Mansoul." Here the whole man receives the message of the Lord, and is comforted thereby. The soul that, having entered into covenant with God, had broken the holy bond; the soul that had neglected the gifts and graces of the Spirit, and entertained the Diabolonians in its bosom; the soul that had been awakened out of this deep slumber, and sought again the presence of the Spirit and the Son; the soul that warred a good warfare in the day of necessity, and had retained the heart as the dwelling-place of an indwelling Christ; to this is the message of peace delivered in the letter of IMMANUEL. And what a change—from darkness to light! So is it ever with the soul that prays persistently, and fainteth not; it shall receive its reward.

> "We kneel, and all around us seems to lower;
> We rise, and all, the distant and the near,
> Stand forth in sunny outline, brave and clear;
> We kneel how weak, we rise how full of power!"

Lord Lieutenant of all the forces.—Faith is, also, a ruling power, a strong captain, a victorious warrior. And now, by reason of him who hath bestowed it, and for its own inherent nature, and for the battles it hath fought, and for the victories it hath won, and for the communion it enjoys with God, it is promoted to the highest place. All the principles of the "new man" are to be under the rule and governance of Faith, and to yield obedience to its command.

Faith empowers all other gifts and graces of the Spirit; it whets the sword, it burnishes the shield, it keeps the Christian armor bright; it nerves the strength; it gives the hope, and earnest, and promise of victory, and even makes us "more than conquerors" at last.

CHAPTER XV

THE PROMISE OF HIS COMING

OUTLINE OF CHAPTER XV.—New Plots and Devices against Mansoul.—Council of War in Hell.—Advice of Apollyon.—Advice of Beelzebub and Lucifer.—A Masterpiece of Hell.—The Counsel of Hell Defeated.—Letter to Captain Credence from Immanuel.—The Promise of his Coming.—Credence consults the Lord Chief Secretary.—The Letter Interpreted.—Reports to the Town.—The Town Rejoices.—The Music of Mansoul.—The Doubters withdraw their Army.—A Pitched Battle.—The Watchword.—The Battle Joined.—Rout and Rally of Diabolus.—The Battle Renewed.—Desperate Conflict; but Immanuel comes not.—The Fight continues; yet Immanuel comes not.—Credence harangues the Army.

A council of war.—The Understanding had already, on behalf of the soul, given back its answer to the demands of DIABOLUS. And now, once more, hell and the grave take counsel together against the striving, struggling, doubting, but still resisting soul. Oh, these awful councils of the pit, these assemblies of the enemies of God and man, when all the varied attributes of the Wicked One meet in conclave, and unite their strength! Every soul that fights and resists is the object of the wrath, and rage, and cunning device of Satan. How largely we need the communion of saints, and, most of all, the communion of the Spirit, to enable us to withstand the communion of devils leagued against the soul!

Withdraw ourselves from the town.—In this hellish council APOLLYON, the great destroyer, speaks. Satan is now represented as dealing with a soul that is hard pressed by the assault of sin, and is at the same time conscious of its danger, and aware of the consequences of yielding to the demands of hell; and one of the devices of the Evil One is to abate the heavy pressure for a season, if haply the soul may again abate its spirit of watchfulness. There are times when the very force of sin and temptation drives the soul more closely to Christ; as when the affrighted sheep has found in the shepherd a refuge from the devouring wolf, and cleaves the closer for the pressing danger. When this is so, the policy of Satan is to lighten the pressure, and to mitigate the force of the temptation, so as once more to allure the soul into lack of vigilance.

To make them sin.—The counsel of BEELZEBUB is superadded to that of the great APOLLYON; and it is a crafty and a wily counsel—to invent a way "to make them sin." Satan knows full well how great an ally he finds in the sin that is done by man. Sin weakens and degrades every power and principle in the soul; it commits the man to the ways of evil, engages him in the service of the Evil One, and ere long binds him captive beneath the hand of the destroyer. Purity and holiness are the strength of the soul; but sin is its weakness. There is no standing fast, no militant spirit as the good soldier of Jesus Christ, where sin is. Sin enervates the soul, prostrates its strength, relaxes its vigor, and casts it down in the helplessness of its weakness, and in the hopelessness of its despair.

Lucifer stood up and said.—The fallen "son of the morning" has also somewhat of advice to offer. The inner counseling mind of Satan is resolved upon the expedient of withdrawing his present force from the soul; but what further measures to adopt he has not yet decided on. The soul is just now in that state that Satan's efforts are calculated rather to alarm than to attract it. The soul is under an awakening, by reason of the very pressure of the heavy hand that is upon it.

Another stratagem.—The soul, if relieved of its present anxiety and alarm, must be engaged and occupied somehow; and this calls forth a new device of Satan—one, however, that he had already tried, and by which he had ere this caused Mansoul to suffer long and deeply. Worldly business, earthly cumber, the preoccupation of the heart and soul with the things that are of the earth, earthy,—these are the main features of this new stratagem. A full market, a busy time, great gain, sudden wealth, fullness of bread, worldly love—these are the things that betray the soul, and bring it into bondage. So said the Church of the Laodiceans—"I am rich, and increased with goods, and have need of nothing," Revelation 3:17. So said the rich man in the parable—"Soul, thou hast much goods laid up for many years; take thine ease, eat, drink, and be merry," Luke 12:19. This is one of the contingencies of earthly circumstances that man does well to pray against—"Lest I be full, and deny thee, and say, Who is the Lord?" Proverbs 30:9.

A warehouse, instead of a garrison.—This is a weighty sentiment, well expressed, and suggestive of many pertinent thoughts. The heart of the renewed man is designed to be an ingarrisoned place, holding within its strong spiritual defenses all the full treasure of the heart, which must not be surrendered, save at the risk of all. Now, if this strong place be filled with earthly treasures, and with carnal things, and with perishable elements, and if from these the carnal desires are fed, and nourished, and supplied, then, indeed, has the man forsaken and forgotten his true position and his proper duty, and thus forfeited the heavenly and abiding treasure, the true riches of the kingdom.

The very masterpiece of hell.—Aye, that it was! No more subtle counsel could have been devised than thus to test the faith of Mansoul in the trying ordeal of worldly prosperity and success. The soul may fight against its doubts, and overcome; it may, by discipline and experience, become a good soldier of Jesus Christ, and yet it might break down under the temptations of Vanity Fair, and witness no good confession when brought to trial before the mammon worshippers that do business there.

Credence received a letter.—"Man's extremity is God's opportunity." In this low estate, God now takes man's part; and in his utter weakness, the Divine hand brings relief. Faith receives a message from its Lord. And this is a message to the soul.

But faith does not always, nor at once, apprehend the full meaning of the Lord's good tidings. It then, for better information, seeks the communion of the Spirit, whose office it is to give a right understanding of the things of God. In this phase of the soul's experience, it is plain the soul was not aware of the danger threatened, and knew nothing respecting this new device of hell. But IMMANUEL knew it all; he knows what we know not; he foresees the danger that we have not yet perceived; he anticipates the counsel of the deep, and comes down to deliver his people from the evil designed against them. The soul has long held out against the assault of the terrible army; it has resisted unto blood; and now that the principles and powers of the soul have bravely and faithfully done their part, Christ will not leave it defenseless in this its sorest strait, and in the day of its greatest danger.

Then were the captains glad.—"All things work together for good to them that love God;" and the soul shall, in due time, reap this goodly consolation, if it faint not. Faith tells the tidings to the heart, and the heart speeds the message, as the life-blood, through the whole man; and all is joy in Mansoul. This is the joy of faith, trusting in the promise of Christ, rejoicing in the great deliverance, glad that the end cometh of all this weary woe and waiting, the end of doubt and fears, the end of night and darkness—by the promise of the sun rising.

What do these madmen mean?—Satan is not all at once made aware of the reasons of the soul's joy and gladness. The message of IMMANUEL reaches the heart of man before it reaches the ear of the Wicked One. Hence, the astonishment of DIABOLUS; it is a marvel and a mystery to him, this joyous blast of the trumpets sounding forth from the castle heights. He can see nothing in the present circum-stances of the soul that should thus be the cause of joy; and he cannot understand how it is that the town, thus fast beleaguered, and already, for the most part, in his hands, should have any occasion for triumph and rejoicing. He knows not yet the secret of Mansoul's joy—how the tidings of IMMANUEL have reached the soul, and the promise of the Prince's coming has rejoiced the heart. And at last he is told the tidings "by one of themselves." Some Diabo-lonian principle, some subdued lust, some carnal desire, feels the presence of "the stronger than he," and reports the discovery to its Diabolonian master.

Best to quit the town.—"Resist the devil, and he will flee from you. Draw nigh to God, and he will draw nigh to you," James 4:7–8. The soul is now experiencing both of these great truths; it has been resisting Satan, and he is now retreating, withdrawing his force from this close and immediate contact with the soul. The approach of Christ involves the departure of Satan, in fear, and trembling, and anticipation of the coming woe.

Experience, ill of his wounds.—The experience of the Christian is subject to casualties; it is a fluctuating element, having its ebb and flow at times; and there are occasions in which it suffers hardly in the battle-field, and is sore wounded. As is the measure of a man's faith, so is the gauge of his experience. When faith fails experience is low and weak; and when faith revives, experience is again quick-ened and refreshed.

Calling for his crutches.—Though experience may be wounded and weak, yet is it minded to work, and willing to engage itself in the good fight of faith. Like READY-TO-HALT in the pilgrim company, he goes forth upon "crutches;" the allusion here being, as it is there, to the "promises" of God. These are the strong support of Christian experience at all times, and especially when it is weak, and sore, and wounded. The promises of God in Christ are sure props to rest upon, when heart and flesh fail us; for then it is that God is felt to be "the strength of our heart, and our portion for ever."

And this assault, on the part of wounded men, alarms Satan more, perhaps, than would the onset of strong men; for he now sees that it can hardly be in their own strength they would thus adven-ture themselves into the battle, and that they must therefore trust to some greater strength than that which is in themselves. And truly so; it is in the strength of the Stronger than man, and the Stronger than Satan, that they fight. "My grace is sufficient for thee, for my strength is made perfect in weakness."

The Prince's army began to faint.—There is faith, but it is faith not yet realized; there is hope, but it is hope as yet deferred, The soul has received the testimony of faith, and so far has believed it as to act upon it; but it needs the assurance of faith and the patience of hope to enable it to endure to the end. The soul fights in faith of a promise—a promise of the intervention of IMMANUEL himself in its behalf; "but no IMMANUEL as yet appeared." This is a test of patience.

A brave speech.—The soul has received the promise of faith in simple trust; and now it needs that faith should still keep the promise alive and fresh in the mind of the soul. Faith must continu-ally speak to man, encourage him, console him, make up for present disappointment, and maintain its own authority to the last. Hence is faith (CREDENCE) represented here as rallying the soul to the last great effort.

And then Immanuel comes.—The promise is sure, and the testimony of faith is true—"Behold, thy King cometh!" This will make amends for all the wounds of the battle-field, for all the loss, for all the woe, for all the pain—the holy Presence of IMMANUEL. "Arise, O Lord, into thy rest; thou, and the ark of thy strength. Let thy priests be clothed with righteousness; and let thy saints shout for joy. . . . For the Lord hath chosen Zion; he hath desired it for his habitation. This is my rest for ever: here will I dwell; for I have desired it. I will abundantly bless her provision: I will satisfy her poor with bread. I will also clothe her priests with salvation: and her saints shall shout aloud for joy. There will I make the horn of David to bud: I have ordained a lamp for mine anointed. His enemies will I clothe with shame: but upon himself shall his crown flourish," Psalm 132:8–9, 13–18.

CHAPTER XVI

RETURN OF THE PRINCE

OUTLINE OF CHAPTER XVI.—Tidings of his Coming.—Renewed Assault.—Credence sees the Approach of the Prince.—Immanuel enters the Battle-field.—The Diabolonians and the Doubters Circumvented.—Enclosed between Immanuel and Captain Credence, they are Defeated (between Christ and Faith, Sin is destroyed).—Mutual Welcomes and Salutations.—Triumphant Entry into Mansoul.—The Order of Procession.—Immanuel receives Mansoul to Himself.—Extermination of Diabolonians.—Mansoul buries the Dead of the Doubters.

One Mr. Speedy.—Mansoul is fighting the good fight of faith. The soul has so far gained advantage, that the army of Doubt has withdrawn itself from the closer contact of an indwelling army of occupation, to the outer plain, the external circumstances and experiences of the soul. An open hand-to-hand encounter is more to be desired than the vexatious conflict with lurking foes, in the dens, and caves, and remote hiding-places of the soul's secret thoughts. Better the pitched battle in the plain than the secret surprise, the guerilla skirmishing, at the hands of every evil thought that suddenly springs up in the heart, to the great detriment of the soul.

Many of the Doubters fell dead.—The nearer the promise, the stronger is the soul, waxing more valiant in fight; and in the same proportion is the power of sin abated, and the force of Satan weakened. Under the increasing evidence of faith, doubt retires, or is beaten back, or is confounded, or is utterly slain. Where faith is strong, and Christ is near, there doubt cannot be in any force or strength against the soul. So now, doubt vanishes as IMMANUEL draws near.

Behold, Immanuel came.—The long-prayed-for issue has arrived. Long and tedious has been the probation of the soul, counting from the day of the departure of the Prince until the day of his return; and what an interval between! The spirit of Carnal-Security has wrought fierce havoc in the soul, involving the withdrawal of

IMMANUEL, the quenching of the SPIRIT, the renewed assault of DIABOLUS, and the countless evils associated with "the terrible army of the Doubters." The soul has renewed its watchfulness, redoubled its prayers, retained possession of the castle (the heart), and, so far, has repulsed the assault and the assailants. But all is incomplete until Christ returns; no full tide of victory till then, nor full deliverance from the power and wrath of Hell. IMMANUEL now comes—"His own arm brought salvation!"

The enemies' place betwixt them.—Between Christ and Faith sin is destroyed. Here is the exercise of human duty, and the intervention of Divine help. This bold coloring of the picture shows what man must do: he must fight, and persevere, and be patient in the strife. It also shows what Christ will do—he will come and crown the fight with victory. His departure was the going forth of the strength of Mansoul from its midst; his return is the renewal of the soul's strength, and health, and well-being. Christ, on one side, slays our doubts, while faith, on the other side, quenches them; and, being thus sore pressed, DIABOLUS, their master, flees from the battle-field, forsakes his terrible army in the crisis of the rout, and takes refuge in the dwelling-place of the abyss of darkness.

His going into Mansoul.—Here is the return of Jesus to the soul. After weary days and tedious years of absence; after deep prostration of the soul, and sorrow of spirit, he now revisits the soul with the pomp of his presence and with the joys of his salvation. Such are the diverse experiences of the soul, as it is *with* Christ or *without* Christ. Mansoul had known and felt the blessedness and happiness of an indwelling Savior. Again, it lost that evidence of spiritual peace, and all was misery, wretchedness, and woe. When Christ departs, doubts arise; the soul is assailed by a thousand fears; terrors and alarms keep it in continual suspense; and all is conflict and encounter. Still the heart holds out for Christ, and this is everything; this retained, all the rest may be regained, and "though heaviness may endure for a night, yet joy cometh in the morning." Here is the wandering soul brought back, the backsliding soul restored, Satan cast out, and Jesus enthroned again. The entry of the Prince is after this "manner and order:"—

1. *With open gates;* to indicate the welcome of the soul to its returning King. The "senses" are now all enlisted in the service of the good Master: Eye-gate is opened, to see his advent, and to welcome him; Ear-gate is unlocked, to hear his blessed words of peace; Mouth-gate is enlarged, to express its gratulation, and to show forth IMMANUEL'S

praise; Feel-gate is all sensitive to his presence; and through its portals joy and gladness thrill throughout the whole man. "Lift up your heads, oh, ye gates!"

2. *With songs of joy;* to show forth the soul's gladness. The pardoned soul is always joyous. There is no peace like that of the soul that is conscious of the Savior's presence and indwelling. "Rejoice in the Lord alway: and again I say, Rejoice," Philippians 4:4.

3. *With a goodly retinue;* forerunners, attendants, and followers. Faith and Hope lead the way—anticipating the advent and manifestation of Christ to the soul; Charity comes behind: an indwelling Christ is always followed by love and good works; and behind all is Patience, willing to wait, and to be last of all. Such are "the things that accompany salvation."

4. *With garlands and flowers;* a further manifestation of the joy and gladness of the now restored soul. The "streets" and "houses" mean all the highways and thoroughfares of man's heart, in which good, and holy, and joyful thoughts abide; and these are foremost in their readiness to receive their Lord. "The shout of a King is in her camp."

5. *With the salutation of the ruling powers;* these had retained the Castle for IMMANUEL; and having fought the good fight, and resisted even unto blood, it is their true joy and gladness to welcome back their Lord to his dwelling-place in the heart. Thus, not only the passing thoughts, but also the abiding principles of the renewed soul are on the side of Christ. The issue of the conflict is the receiving back of IMMANUEL to the soul.

6. *With the submission of the inferior powers;* the lower principles of the soul are subordinated to the governance of Christ. The passions, the desires, the appetites are all brought to his feet, and own allegiance to their sovereign Lord. The whole man is subjected to the yoke of Christ.

I am returned with mercies.—Well might the prayer of Mansoul be— "Enter not into judgment with thy servant, O Lord!" and here the Lord proclaims himself to be, as of old, "the Lord merciful and gracious." In the abundance of his mercies he has returned to Mansoul— to bless and not to curse, to comfort and not to vex, to reward and not to punish. New badges of his love, new tokens of his affection, new symbols of his full pardon are now bestowed upon the soul. "In the joy of the Lord is thy strength!"

"Wash your garments."—After the soul's relapse and backsliding, many duties remain to be done. Guilt has been more or less contracted,

the garments have been more or less stained and spotted with the flesh, and Christian purity contaminated. All must now be restored, in fullness, in holiness, in peace. When Mansoul had been first invested with the pure white garments, it was with the charge to "keep them clean;" and if, peradventure, any spot or stain should be contracted, to go forthwith and wash them in the fountain of cleansing. The soul *has* contracted defilement, and *has* stained her garments, oft and oft during the sad interval of Immanuel's absence; but now she washes and makes them clean in the pure waters of the fountain of the sanctifying Spirit.

Pursued them night and day.—How hard it is utterly to destroy sin! After the most searching investigation, after a spiritual conflict of many years' continuance, after the battle of the warrior, and even after a triumphant issue, it is yet necessary to search, and try, and examine the soul, and to "pursue" the evil that still cleaveth to the flesh. The Will of even the renewed man has this burden laid upon it, thus to quench every rising thought of evil, and to uproot every living seed of sin. Not otherwise is the carnal nature subdued and kept under.

To bury the dead.—The army of Doubt is destroyed; a complete rout has covered them with shame, defeat, and ruin. But the Christian soldier has not yet done all, until the very bodies of the dead are buried out of his sight. Sins are defiling and contaminating under any circumstances. The least remnant or remembrance of sin is fraught with danger to the soul. Sin must not only be slain, but it must also be buried. Thus we found in the "Pilgrim's Progress" that the burden of sin, when unloosed from the shoulders of the Pilgrim, did fall into the "sepulchre." There, in the grave, is pardoned sin buried, and forgotten; and there is no resurrection of buried sin. Thus does the renewed soul seek to compass the utter extermination of the Doubters.

Such was the day of the conflict—so sharp and so severe the battle of the warrior; but now is the day of the triumph, when this "terrible army" is routed and slain, and even the dead of the Doubters are buried. This episode of the soul's history describes one phase of the spiritual fight; another will follow immediately after. All are designed to teach the Christian man that his path is a difficult path, his state a militant state, and that his strength, and hope, and joy, and crown of rejoicing are only to be found in the continued presence of Immanuel.

CHAPTER XVII

THE ARMY OF BLOOD-MEN

OUTLINE OF CHAPTER XVII.—Return of Diabolus and Incredulity to their Den.—Renewed Council of War.—A new Expedition against Mansoul.—The Blood-men.—The Conjoined Army of Doubters and Blood-men.—The Captains, Standard-bearers, and Escutcheons.—Mr. Prywell again.—Message of Mansoul to the Prince.—The Answer.—The Siege.—The Battle.—Capture of the Blood-men.—Their Trial and Examination.—Whence they came.—Their Sentence.

Blood-men.—This new device of Satan means the enterprise of persecution and the wrath of persecutors. Having tried the power and efficacy of doubt against the soul, he would now bring the power of persecution against the body, to see whether the external agency of fire, and sword, and fagot might not prove more efficacious than the internal exercise and struggle of the soul against the army of doubt.

Persecution is generally the last resort of a bad cause. When men have resisted arguments and entreaties, and have stood firm against all the efforts that address themselves to the reason, the understanding, or the feelings, then it is that the secular arm is put forth, and the hand of power is laid to the hilt of the sword, and right is opposed and antagonized by might.

So was it in the days of the Reformation, and so we must with sorrow confess it continued in a measure to be, even in the later age when Bunyan lived. The doubting and oft-despairing Bunyan was also the afflicted and oft-persecuted Bunyan. Such persecution as his pilgrim heroes suffered in Vanity Fair is here introduced as part of the trial and probation of Mansoul—imprisonment and death. And not infrequently has the power of bodily persecution brought the man to a break-down, who has boldly held on to his protest in the face of spiritual assaults. So, on this occasion, after doubt has been repelled, is the weapon of persecution tried.

This peculiar phase of the soul's peril is as clearly and elaborately developed by Bunyan's pen as any other of his inimitable descriptions. For example, the names of the captains of the army of Blood-men are suggestive, embodying those names which are in Holy Scripture, or in human history, associated with rapine, hatred, and bloodshed; such as CAIN, who slew his brother, the first martyr to the witness of truth; NIMROD; the mighty hunter, the beginning of whose kingdom was Babel, commenced in presumption, and ended in confusion; ISHMAEL, the scorner of the holy seed, the vagrant of the desert, a man of blood—"his hand against every man, and every man's hand against him;" ESAU, who hated his brother, and thirsted for his blood; SAUL, with his malice and envy against David, the chosen of the Lord; ABSALOM, the type of those men who would persecute even their own flesh, recognizing no tie of affection, no claim of relationship, no bond of brotherhood or sonship; JUDAS, with the blood-money of the traitor, who sold his Master; and POPE, well worthy of a place amid the chief persecutors, and well described by the device upon the escutcheon of his standard-bearer—"The stake, the flame, and the good man in it!"

Mr. Prywell.—The same principle—self-examination—that discovered the former plot, is again represented as guarding the interests of the soul on this occasion. Here it would be the inner conscience and firm persuasion of the soul, abundantly convinced that the part it has chosen is "the good part;" so that though bonds and affliction await the man of God, he knows in whom he has believed, and is prepared to abide the consequences of the profession and possession of the faith of Christ. The martyrs of the Church of Christ were men whose convictions were strong, whose faith was firm, whose love was earnest, and whose consistency was steadfast, even unto death. Their self-examination—inquiry as to their faith, hope, and love, rendered them proof against the doubts that assailed the feelings (Feel-gate). The instruments of torture, that were exposed before their view (Eye-gate), and the tempting or taunting words that were addressed to their hearing (Ear-gate), were powerless to withdraw them from the testimony of Jesus.

Captain Self-Denial.—In the face of threatening danger, there is no more effective ally to the soul than the principle of self-denial. Self-indulgence is not the spirit of martyrs; it needs a stronger principle to enable a man to resist the blood-men of persecution.

Self-denial is the discipline of the Christian man; he has to fight the good fight, therefore he must be bred and inured to hardships; he has to sail the voyage of life, and must therefore be strong to face the tempests, and brave the billows of the deep. Self-denial is the medicine of the soul—not always sweet, but most frequently bitter. Self-denial is the foundation of manly heroism and of all heroic virtues—"seeking not her own." This is a cross-bearing place, even to the mount of sacrifice. Self-denial thinks more of tomorrow's sunshine than of the tempest of today. It provides for the time to come at the cost of the time now present; and walks by faith of future glory, and not by sight of present suffering—"choosing rather to suffer affliction—having respect unto the recompense of the reward." Martyrs have always been self-denying men.

The Doublers made a retreat.—Once routed before, they are now routed again. When Faith, Hope, and Experience are strong in the soul, doubt cannot stand; and these were now the brave defenders of Mansoul.

The Blood-men also.—The inward sins are to be utterly slain; not so the outward agents of persecution—they are reserved, some for repentance, some for a season of better knowledge, and some for the judgment of God, who alone is the umpire of men's deeds and destinies.

And at this point is described an instructive episode of the con-flict, illustrative of the nature and character of the persecuting spirit in man. It arises from three sources: (1) from *ignorance;* (2) from *blind zeal;* and (3) from *malice* and *envy.* And each of these is to be diversely dealt with—"Of some have compassion, making a difference," Jude 22.

1. There are those who persecute in *ignorance.* Such were even some of the persecutors of our Lord, and hence his dying prayer—"Father, forgive them; for they know not what they do," Luke 23:34. For such as these there is mercy. Hence the dying prayer of the martyr Stephen—"Lay not this sin to their charge," Acts 7:60. Saul of Tarsus was also one of this class, for he says of himself, "Who was before a blasphemer, and a persecutor, and injurious: but I obtained mercy, because I did it ignorantly in unbelief," 1 Timothy 1:13.

2. Those who are influenced by *blind zeal.* These are alluded to by our blessed Lord, when he said to his disciples, "Yea, the time cometh, that whosoever killeth you will think that he doeth God service;" and this would arise from spiritual blindness; for he adds, "And these things will they do unto you, because they have not known the Father, nor me," John 16:2–3. This is that sort of zeal of which the Apostle speaks, as being "not according to knowledge."

3. Persecutors who are influenced by *malice.* These are the guilty persecutors, whose spirit comes of *sin.* These know the truth, but

hate it; see the light, but come not to it; and with malice prepense pursue good men to death. These are they who seek to fulfill their lust of blood upon the servants of the Most High—the Blood-men of the past history of the Church and people of God. Well did the soul cry out to the Prince against this danger, "Lord, save Mansoul from bloody men!"

CHAPTER XVIII

TAKE HEED! MANSOUL

OUTLINE OF CHAPTER XVIII.—A New Conspiracy.—Promoted by
Mr. Evil-Questioning.—The League with the Doubters.—Discovered
by Mr. Diligence.—Report to Willbewill.—Seizure of Doubters and
Diabolonians.—Trial of Evil-Questioning.—Denies his Name.—The
Witnesses.—His Condemnation.—Trial of the Doubters.—Their
Condemnation.—The Execution.—Further Search for Diaboloni-
ans.—All is Peace in Mansoul.

Evil-Questioning.—Notwithstanding the signal defeat of the conjoined army of Doubters and Blood-men, the wrath of hell is still
busy with new plots and fresh designs against the soul. Insatiable
indeed is the gorge of hell, and inventive the capacity of the Evil
One in the devices of his cruel wrath against the man of God. Satan
hungers and thirsts for souls. The "terrible army" of Doubt has been
routed; the army of Blood-men has been reserved for the future
decision of the Judge; and yet it would appear there are doubts
enough yet lingering about for the purpose of making further
attempts to overcome the fidelity and consistency of the child of
God. Again and again, in Bunyan's own experience, did these doubts
and fears come forth "from the land of Doubting," tending to entangle the soul, and plunge it in deeper perplexity.

The form that this present phase of peril assumes, is that of
doubt arising in the soul from the spirit of evil-questioning. This is
not the spirit of legitimate inquiry, nor of diligent self-examination,
but rather a spirit of unbelief, engendered in the soul by the encouragement of morbid doubts, as indicated by the names of the
Doubters here referred to, which signify a revival of those doubts
which question God's electing love, his effectual call, the fullness of
salvation, and that all is of God's good grace and mercy.

Bunyan here speaks experimentally; for even in his converted
state he was sorely tried by such doubts as these. For example, in
his "Grace Abounding" he records how the "*Election* doubters" and
the "*Grace* doubters," as he here calls them, vexed his soul:—"Here I

began to find my soul to be assaulted with fresh doubts about my future happiness; especially with such as these, Whether I was elected? But how, if the day of grace should now be past and gone?" And again, he speaks of the "*Vocation* doubters:"—"Here I was at a very great stand, not knowing what to do, fearing I was not *called;* for, thought I, if I be not called, what then can do me good?"

Talk not too loud.—There are times when doubts may wax presumptuous in the soul; but it behooves them to speak with bated breath when the Spirit and Immanuel are enshrined within. It is as it were by stealth and secretly that any such doubt can be entertained and encouraged in the soul when Jesus reigns supreme.

Willbewill.—This brave minister of the King still holds his all-important office in the renewed man. It is the duty of the watchful, sanctified, militant Will of man to search out and destroy these doubts that gather round the soul, as the billows in the deep, or as the breakers on the shore. These doubts are not to be entertained, are not to be indulged; but must be bravely and stoutly, as on this occasion, resisted by the strong hand and sturdy arm of the Will.

Mr. Diligence.—When the Will of the renewed man is seconded by diligence in search and action, all is well for the soul's health and well-being. Something like Mr. Prywell is this trusty servant of the sanctified Will, Mr. Diligence. He goes up and down, and to and fro, in the soul, searching out the lurking power of evil. Bunyan means by this to lay repeated honor on the principle of self-examination. It is well for the soul when it is thus watchful and diligent, and prompt in giving information; and when the Will is strong and resolute to act upon the information given.

Bring them forth to public judgment.—As in a former phase of the soul's history, so on this occasion it is necessary to bring the Diabolonian principles to judgment, and, after condemnation, to execution. It is, indeed, a similar process of the soul's discipline; for the same principles as sat in judgment on the former trial are empanelled now to try the evil-questioning of the soul.

The Indictment.—A charge is preferred against the lurking spirit of evil, that it exists but for the disturbance of the soul's peace, and for the encouragement of the soul's enemies. There can be no joy, no peace, no growth in grace, no abounding of the fruit of righteousness, while the foundations are thus exposed to danger by the sapping and mining process of the doubts and cavils of Mr. Evil-Questioning.

The Defense.—Here is a very instructive illustration of the plea set up by false principles in self-defense: they seek to screen themselves from conviction and condemnation by denying their true name, and by assuming a name more plausible than genuine. How many a man is plunged in hopeless doubt and difficulty by allowing himself to think that he is conducting an *honest inquiry* in spiritual things, while all the time he is indulging the dangerous principle of *evil-questioning!* It is thus that souls are shaken in their faith, and at last ensnared in the bondage of skepticism and unbelief.

The Evidence.—This is elicited by the testimony of "two witness- es"—Lord WILLBEWILL and Mr. DILIGENCE. The Will of man is, indeed, enabled to speak from experience to the identity of this evil principle of the carnal nature; for in days gone by, days of past ungodliness, the Will had consorted with Evil-Questioning, had entertained it, indulged it, and made it to feel a welcome in Mansoul. The Will remembers this with shame, and bears witness to it. Thus is the spiritual will able to detect the rising evil, by calling to mind the experience of its former influence in the day of its power. The dili- gence of the soul is also able to testify against the evil principle: the diligent eye of the soul has seen its corrupt doings; the diligent ear of the soul has heard its words of treason; the diligent understanding of the soul has followed all its treacherous correspondence and commu- nication; and the diligent hand of the soul has laid hold of the Diabo- lonian agent, to bind it in chains, and lead it forth to judgment. And the witness of WILLBEWILL and DILIGENCE is true.

The Sentence.—The Understanding sits in judgment on the Diabo- lonian principle, and from the evidence of the Will, and of the self- examination of the soul, it decrees the sentence of death against this troubler of the peace of Mansoul. Its "questionings" were traitors, whose only object was to undermine the soul's faith, and trust, and loyalty toward its King. As such, this principle is adjudged to die the death.

The Election Doubter.—There is such a thing as "the election of God." However deep and mysterious it may seem, it yet is true that "whom he did foreknow, he also did predestinate to be conformed to the image of his Son," Romans 8:29. To doubt, or to deny this, is to doubt or to deny the omniscience of Jehovah, the all-potency of his will, and the irresistible character of his decrees—"for who hath resisted his will?" God is the sovereign Lord and Master; he must be permitted to do as he will with his own; so that salvation shall be regarded as being altogether of God's own will, and according to his free grace. "So then it is not of him that willeth, nor of him that runneth, but of God that showeth mercy," Romans 9:16.

The Vocation Doubter.—There is the effectual calling of God, by which he awakes the sleeping soul, raises the dead soul, calls the wandering soul, and thus brings home to the soul the great purpose of his electing love—"Whom he did predestinate, them he also called," Romans 8:30. This "call" of God is effected sometimes by the ministry of his servants, sometimes by the preaching of his Word, sometimes by the agency of his providence, and always by the influence of his Holy Spirit directly acting upon the soul, or indirectly through the instrumentality of outward circumstances.

The Grace Doubter.—All is of grace. "Salvation is of the Lord." It is not of human works, not of human merit, but altogether of Divine grace, that we are saved. "By grace are ye saved through faith; and that not of yourselves: it is the gift of God," Ephesians 2:8. Truly does the "grace doubter" come of the race of Pharisees, who glory in the deeds of the flesh! The spirit of human pride would resist this truth, and glory in the flesh, and in the deeds of the law. But salvation cannot otherwise be than through sovereign grace and of undeserved mercy. Of the "sons of God" it is written—"Which were born, not of blood, nor of the will of the flesh, nor of the will of man, but of God," John 1:13.

The Execution.—These doubts must be utterly slain. Like all other Diabolonian or hellish principles, they must be brought to the Cross, and there crucified. With an unsparing hand they must be dealt with; else with an unsparing hand will they deal with us. If they are not mortified, they will slay us. The Cross is the place at which to "crucify the old man," with its affections and lusts, with its doubts and evil-questionings.

Had thus far rid themselves.—This is, indeed, a holy warfare of the soul. This is the resolute discipline of the man of God, who is strong in the Lord and in the power of his might. The active searching of the heart for the discovery of one particular evil principle, may lead to the discovery of many lurking foes. Sins abide in families, in circles; and the finding of one may involve the existence of many. And as the soul is strong to discover and slay one particular sin, so will it become yet more strong to discover more, and utterly to slay them all.

Accordingly this is now a season of the soul's peculiar watchfulness and diligence; it is one of the later stages of its eventful history, when it is growing in grace, increasing in wisdom, enlarging in experience, and ripening for eternal glory. The things of the flesh are now dying within her, and the things of the Spirit are living and growing in her. Every rising thought of evil is checked; every budding forth of the corrupt nature is nipped; and the whole body of sin is mortified.

Hence the signal success of the soul's search after indwelling sin; and the faithfulness of the soul in dealing with discovered sin. Hence, too, the long catalogue of the slain—the evil things that lurk the longest, and linger to the last, in Mansoul, tending so mightily to retard the onward progress of the soul to God. This is a description of the thorough subjugation of the "old man" to the new nature; the full dominion of Christ, who is all in all. Some sins are slain outright, and so put out of the way; some are bound in prison, and so restrained; some pine away for lack of nurture and encouragement; but *all* are, at last, utterly destroyed. The soul is watchful, and most sensitive to the least suspicion of sin. The thoughts, the hopes, the joys, the feelings, are all jealously alive to the least sign, or token, or returning symptom of the revival of any sin, or of any love of sin in the heart or flesh.

And then is the high festival of the soul's peace, and joy, and rejoicing. IMMANUEL now abides in the soul, and reveals himself, and makes all his goodness to pass before it. It is all his own, and he will honor it. He will bless it, and make it holy, and make it happy. He will arm it, and strengthen it, and advise it, and protect it. And even now he prepares to speak to it words of peace. When Satan is utterly cast out, then does Christ enter in with all his power; and as the last remnant of the root of sin is plucked up, so does Christ take root in the heart, and fill it with his own great Presence, and inspire it with his Spirit, and refresh it with his love.

CHAPTER XIX

IMMANUEL'S ADDRESS TO MANSOUL

OUTLINE OF CHAPTER XIX.—Immanuel meets the Townsmen.—
His Address.—Declares his Love, his Sacrifice, his Longsuffering,
his Providence, his Pardon and Forgiveness, his Indwelling Power.—Mansoul shall yet be Transplanted to a fairer Land.—The
Glories of that Land.—Present Duties; must keep her Garments
white and clean; must show forth her Love towards God, must be
watchful, and remember the Past.—"Remember, therefore, O my
Mansoul; hold fast till I come!"

The Prince appointed a day.—It would seem as though the soul, as
here described, had now arrived at that happy state of communion
with God which is called, in the Pilgrim's Progress, the Land of
Beulah. The warfare is so far fought, and victory has crowned the
faithful struggle of the soul. And now it rests, and is at peace, and
bathes its weary frame in the ocean of the all-gracious love of Him
for whom the fight has hitherto been waged. The man of God now
sits in full view of Christ his Savior, and listens to his voice, and
holds sweet communion with the Spirit; and the comforts of the
Lord are for the refreshing of his soul. This communion of the soul
with God is now described by Bunyan in this the finishing stroke of
the Holy War.

You, my Mansoul.—Christ addresses the soul as being *his own.* The
soul is his by creation, by preservation, and, most of all, by redemption.
And in this consists the safety and security of the people of God—"Ye
are not your own; for ye are bought with a price," 1 Corinthians 6:19–
20. Hence does God claim the renewed soul, calling it "mine," and
valuing it as some precious and costly treasure—"And they shall be
mine, saith the Lord of hosts, in that day when I make up my jewels,"
Malachi 3:17. He speaks to the soul as to a delivered captive, a pardoned rebel, a lost one reclaimed, a prodigal restored. And this restora-
tion has been altogether of God's love; this love produced the sacrifice
of Jesus; this sacrifice was a satisfaction, full and for ever; and through
this satisfaction the soul is reconciled unto God.

He furthermore tells what was the process by which this great work was accomplished. First, by the Law, the stern and rough-hewn Captains of the first campaign. Secondly, by the Gospel, the next great enterprise of Heaven in the interest of the soul, accompanied by the virtues and graces of the Spirit. And lastly, by the continuous discipline of the soul—God's dealings with the sinful soul, with the repentant soul, with the renewed soul, with the backsliding soul, and at last with the reinstated soul. And when the conquest was gained, and the victory won, it was turned altogether to the advantage of the soul. For this reason the discipline was sustained, and the heart possessed by the army of occupation, that Man might be made meet for heaven. It was God's hand throughout, from first to last—reproving, rebuking, chastising, testing, and thus preparing the soul for himself, and for the enjoyment of eternal glory.

For yet a little while.—All the past is thus made plain and clear; and all the future is full of like blessed dealings of God with the soul, resulting in a final transplanting of Mansoul to a fairer clime and to a happier land. In the prospect of death, Christ will gather the soul, and in the resurrection he will gather the body, to the house of many mansions—"Mine own country, even the kingdom of my Father." The renewed soul is but an exotic here; but the day shall come when the goodly plant shall be transferred, by the hand of the great Husband-man, from the chill, cold atmosphere of earth, its place of exile, to heaven, its native dwelling-place. And this final transplanting shall be a triumphant scene; not with sorrows, and partings, and rendings, but in resurrection joy, and in eternal glory. Angels shall be the reapers of the goodly harvest, the bearers of the garnered grain; their bosoms as the chariots of the Lord; their wings as the car of triumph, upbearing the ransomed ones to their eternal home!

And now, thy duty and practice.—Still is Mansoul in the flesh; and, though clothed upon with holy garments, yet must the soul walk amid the multitude, and through the unclean places of this naughty world. It must, therefore, be careful to keep its garments white and clean. It must oft repair to the cleansing fountain. The saints of the Lord must needs be white-robed even here—"known and read of all men;" receiving light and reflecting light; witnessed to by the effectu-al working of the Spirit, and thus witnessing the indwelling power and presence of the Holy Ghost.

And the warfare must still, in a measure, continue; the Canaan-ite is still in the land. There can be no discharge from this war, until death releases us from duty, and introduces us to glory. There must be no sheathing of the sword, so long as a single enemy remains to be overcome, or a single foot of land to be attained. We fight until we conquer.

Our work is done; our reading of this wondrous Allegory is ended; another rich treasure is cast into our bosom; another talent committed to our trust.

We have thus been enabled to trace the "History of the Soul" throughout its varied stages, its alternations, its vicissitudes, its sunshine and its tears, its night of darkness and its noontide glory. All sorts of spiritual experience are included here—the willing service of Satan's bond-slaves, the rebellion of the disobedient sons, the sorrows of the soul's captivity, the alarms of a troubled conscience, the betaking of the soul to God in penitence and prayer, the return of the prodigal to his Father, the submission of the rebel to his King, the pleasantness of religious ways, the backsliding of transgressors, the hardening of the heart, the carnal security of the soul, the awakening of the soul to a consciousness of its danger, its cry to the Mighty for help, the long and weary discipline, the seeking back to God, the finding of the lost and loved One, the renewal of the holy allegiance and sonship, and the loving and affectionate counsel of the great IMMANUEL!

MANSOUL LOST

"LET us make man," Jehovah said,
And in His image Man was made.
A Son of God, an heir of Heaven,
All God-like gifts to him were given.

His Body was the meet abode
And temple of the Living God.
His Soul, the sacred inner shrine,
Filled with the Presence all Divine.

'Twas then that Hell occasion sought,
And deeds of ruin Satan wrought.
The chariot-wheels of Tophet roll
Against the fortress of Mansoul.

It yields—and swift destruction falls
Upon its battlements and walls.
The citizens their King disown,
And Sin usurps the fallen throne.

Upborne to heaven the echoes rise,
Wafted from earth to yonder skies.
"*My* blood, *my* life," Immanuel saith,
"Shall rescue Mansoul from this death!"

MANSOUL REGAINED

Down from His throne of peace and love,
Down from the shining seats above,
He came—He died—by sovereign grace
To purchase back the rebel race.

It is a warfare sore and long,
And Hell's permitted strength is strong;
And souls are lost, and conquests won—
But yet Immanuel marches on!

My soul! He seeks thy throne to gain,
To wield the sceptre of his reign.
All earth and Heaven are bound in this,
Thy peace and future happiness!

Open thine ears to hear His word;
Open thine eyes to see the Lord.
Hold fast the royal courtly dress,
Keep clean the Robe of Righteousness!

"I ask thy heart—oh, give it Me!
And thou, my Mansoul, shalt be free
Once more the sacred inner shrine,
Redeem'd, restor'd—FOR EVER MINE!"

Manufactured by Amazon.ca
Bolton, ON